Talking to Alzheimer's *addresses head on both the practical and emotional difficulties experienced by loved ones and the effort it takes to respond as lovingly and constructively as possible when visiting. Strauss' approach is appropriately person-centered and validating: the only way to constructively interact with a person in the grip of dementia. Full of examples of what to do and say and what not to do and say, this is a valuable handbook to which a person can return again and again.*

> —John A. Jager, MSW, Executive Director
> of the Alzheimer's Association, New York
> City Chapter

Strauss' book is all about hope. It reminds us to look at the person with Alzheimer's disease holistically and not focus only on the dementia. She offers suggestions that will enrich people's lives and preserve dignity.

> —Kara P. Ray, R.N., Corporate Director of
> The Meadows Program, the Alzheimer's care
> program of Country Meadows Retirement
> Communities

This is practical, a kind of 'how to' discussion that is easy to read and understand. It is in the 'must buy' category. Any organization specializing in the promotion of optimal care for the demented should find this sourcebook valuable. So should family members and potential volunteers in the community.

> —William H. Reifsnyder, M.D., Medical
> Director, The Highlands of Wyomissing,
> A Life-Care Retirement Community

Ms. Strauss gives page after page of specific advice to the reader, and I repetitively found myself wondering, 'Why hadn't I thought of that?' This book would be a welcome addition to any physician's waiting room.

—Peter A. Schwartz, M.D., Director,
Department of Obstetrics and Gynecology,
Reading Hospital and Medical Center

Talking to Alzheimer's fills a major void in our knowledge. I found that this book significantly altered my conception of the problem and my ability and willingness to deal in a meaningful way with Alzheimer patients. I enthusiastically recommend this book to physicians of any discipline who encounter such patients in their practice, as well as to laymen who have family members or friends facing this devastating illness.

—E. Berry Hey, Jr., M.D., Senior Physician,
Reading Hospital and Medical Center

This book recognizes that families need to rethink and rework what is meant by meaningful communication when faced with loved ones who suffer from dementia. Strauss unearths myriad possibilities for effective open-ended communication, provides detailed pointers on how to navigate through this territory, and shows the potential for sharing the joy of a profound human connection. Talking to Alzheimer's is designed to be used for hands-on help. But it is also a compassionate book that helps both friends and relatives make more meaningful connections under these new and constantly changing conditions."

—Nancy J. Brooks, Alzheimer's family member,
and health, rehabilitation and social work
professional

TALKING to ALZHEIMER'S

Simple Ways to Connect
When You Visit with a
Family Member or Friend

CLAUDIA J. STRAUSS

Foreword by Zaven S. Khachaturian, Ph.D.

NEW HARBINGER PUBLICATIONS, INC.

Publisher's Note

This publication is designed to provide accurate and authoritative information in regard to the subject matter covered. It is sold with the understanding that neither the publisher nor the author is engaged in rendering psychological, financial, legal, or other professional services. This work expresses the author's opinions and experiences and is not intended to provide and does not provide either psychological or medical advice. If expert assistance or counseling is needed, the services of a competent professional should be sought.

Distributed in Canada by Raincoast Books

Copyright © 2001 by Claudia J. Strauss
New Harbinger Publications, Inc.
5674 Shattuck Avenue
Oakland, CA 94609

Cover design by Salmon Studios
Edited by Brady Kahn
Book design by Michele Waters

ISBN-10 1-57224-270-1
ISBN-13 978-1-57224-270-8

New Harbinger Publications' Web site address:
www.newharbinger.com

08   07   06

20   19   18   17   16   15   14   13   12   11

People need joy
quite as much as clothing.
Some of them need it
far more.

—Margaret Collier Graham

For J.T.

I also dedicate this book to all the people who face this painful, wasting disease; to all those who live with it, experience it, witness it; to all those who struggle with the loss of control over words, over memory, over meaning; to all those who face the tearing apart of relationships, the tearing down of identity, the disintegration of the tools of communication and bonding that we usually rely on.

And I dedicate this book to all the people who want to strengthen their relationships, continue to bring joy to those they love, and focus on the essence that makes them who they are.

Contents

Acknowledgments

I would like to express my unending thanks and gratitude to those who have supported me in writing this book, and have given of their time and experience to read, to comment, to suggest, to test, and to validate what is offered here. So many have helped me along the way that there's no way to thank all of you here. I would particularly like to thank Karen Kelsey, who supports me in all my endeavors; M.H., who took a great interest and made many valuable suggestions; Nancy Brooks, who contributed from a wealth of personal experience; Kara Ray, R.N., Marie Amoroso, and others on the staffs of the Meadows and Meadows Plus units at Country Meadows Retirement Communities who provided valuable feedback; Dr. Peter Schwartz, director of the Department of Obstetrics and Gynecology, Reading Hospital, who read the manuscript with an attention to detail; and Dr. Bill Reifsnyder, medical director of The Highlands of Wyomissing, a Continuing Care Retirement Community, who made many suggestions about its application. Without you, this book would not exist.

I would also like to thank those of you who believed in this book and helped bring it to other people's hands: Joe Brancatelli, Steve Ferber, Bill Kaye, John Jager, Jill Einstein, Lisa Gwyther, Joan Davis, Howard Gardner, Ellen Winner, Marion Gardner

Saxe, Kathy Hourigan, and Jonathan Kozol. Your belief helped transform the manuscript into this book.

That transformation was promoted and shepherded by Jim Levine, my agent, and by the people at New Harbinger: Jueli Gastwirth, Heather Garnos Mitchener, and Brady Kahn, my editors; Amy Shoup and Michele Waters, who created the cover and interior design; and Lauren Dockett and the other members of the marketing team. Their vision in seeing the need for this book, and their passion in moving it through the process, made everything crystallize.

I would particularly like to thank Zaven Khachaturian and Dr. Peter Rabins for their support in getting this book to the people it is intended to help.

Many people contributed to this book without ever knowing they were doing so. I'd like to name some of them here: Leona, Marion, Gertrude, Lillian, Doris, John, Frank, Mary, Marie, Dorothy, Rose, Ervin, Margaret, Lou, Geraldine, Lena, Lois, Violet, Elda, Christine, Catherine, Katrina, Betty, Florence, Ruth, Edith, Josephine, Loretta, and Bill. This book is for you.

Other people contributed to this book without knowing it, and they are on the front lines of providing loving attention, daily care, and respect: Kelly, Jason, Flor, Susan, Lucy, Blossom, Laurie, Helen, Dolores,

Andrea, Shirley, Felicita, Judy, Idalis, Karlene, and many others like you everywhere. Thank you.

There are two other groups I'd like to thank. First, those of you who helped me develop the short list of resources found at the back of this book: John Jager, MSW, Executive Director of the NYC Chapter of the Alzheimer's Association; Lisa Gwyther, LCSW, Director of the Family Caregiver Support Program at Duke University Medical Center; Lisa Snyder, LCSW, of the University of California, San Diego Alzheimer's Disease Research Center; Joan Davis, Chairman of the board of the National Capital Area Chapter of the Alzheimer's Association; Betty Ransom, Director of Education and training of the National Capital Area Chapter; and Karin Udler, LCSW, Help Line Manager, National Capital Area Chapter.

And I'd also like to thank the people who are always there to encourage me, believe in me, and support me: Dale Broman, Nancy Knoblauch, Marlene Fedin, Frank and Eva Schaal, Diana Grass, Harry Weilheimer, my friends Howard and Ethel, my incomparable cousin Hilde Gardner, my uncle George, my brothers, and my mother, Lore Strauss.

I am grateful to everyone who has been supportive, whether listed here or not, for their faith in me and their many contributions. Thank you.

Foreword

Talking to Alzheimer's is a welcome addition to the growing knowledge base on how to communicate and cope with the person who has the disease. This volume provides practical guidance in communication skills to help families, caregivers, professionals, and others who might interact with people gradually losing their cognitive abilities.

One of the distinguishing features of this book is its dual emphasis. It focuses on the dignity of the person with Alzheimer's as well as on the continuing potential for mutually rich relationships. In doing that, it supports both the person with the disease and the people involved in visiting and care. There are numerous examples of how to create warmth, meaningful conversations, and close connections. Using these approaches will not only reduce stress for everyone involved in this difficult situation, but will also increase the amount and frequency of positive mental stimulation. That this contributes to happier and healthier lives and helps to sustain cognitive abilities is beginning to be recognized.

Although Alzheimer's disease was described nearly one hundred years ago, knowledge about diagnosis, possible causes, treatments, and the care of people with the disease was slow in developing. Throughout the history of the disease, the concept of "senility" has been the most persistent, though unproven idea—the idea that Alzheimer's was an inevitable consequence of aging.

Until recently, Alzheimer's was dismissed as an untreatable disorder, and the strategy of care consisted of custodial services in environments that were essentially warehouses. However, since the 1980s, largely due to the public awareness campaign of the Alzheimer's Association and the increasing support for research on behavioral, social, and environmental aspects of the disease, attitudes have begun to change.

It is now evident that, although the biology of neurodegeneration gradually plunders the cognitive abilities of the person with the disease, the strategies of care and the communication skills of the care provider could help to maintain independent functioning and life with dignity, and slow the rate of losses in the activities of daily living. This accessible and compassionate volume by Claudia Strauss provides a unique perspective on how to communicate to achieve these goals, and fills a gap that needed to be filled. It is a valuable contribution to the field of care for dementia, which has yet so much to learn.

—Zaven S. Khachaturian, Ph.D.
Senior Medical & Science Advisor,
Alzheimer's Association
Former Director, Office of Alzheimer's
Research, National Institute on
Aging, National Institutes of Health

Preface

Though this book may appear to be for friends and family visiting loved ones suffering from Alzheimer's and related conditions, it is also intended for those who have both time and love to give to strangers.

I hope this book will help all kinds of visitors, coming for all sorts of reasons, to have rewarding visits and rich relationships. Those who start by visiting strangers will be surprised to find a new family inside unfamiliar walls.

Because most of the book speaks more directly to family and friends, I'd like to devote this space to those who volunteer and visit.

I came to this by accident. My son was part of a group providing entertainment in an assisted-living unit. I stood in the doorway and talked with a woman who couldn't bring herself to go in, yet couldn't bring herself to leave, either. She stood poised on the threshold. We had the same conversation thirty times over the next hour. What struck me about this woman was her dignity in the face of fear. There was no doubt she was frightened. No doubt she was confused. She didn't know how to get home, and wasn't sure she had a place to stay for the night. Yet she was calm, kept a smile on her face, and observed all the social niceties. I felt this was a person worth knowing. When I asked a staff member if it would be all right to visit her, and then checked with her to see if she would welcome that, a process started that eventually led to this book.

There has been a lot to learn along the way, and times when I struggled, but there have been many times when I have walked out the door thinking that I've gotten at least as much out of the visit as the people I visited. On some days, it seems like more.

For many of us, whose lives are full, squeezing in some extra time turns out to be a bonus. For others of us, finding a need we can meet fills empty spaces. Some of us face empty nests; others lose children for other reasons; some retire from work with a lot of energy and purpose to spare. Whether you are busy or not, hurting or not, lonely or not, bored or not, or spilling over with happiness—you will be welcome if you come openly, lovingly, and with patience.

What you find cannot be measured.

Introduction

This book came out of a need I saw when visiting people in a locked unit. I found that I wasn't sure how to handle a number of situations, and that there wasn't really anywhere I could go to get answers and advice. I also noticed how few visitors came and how they seemed to be struggling with these same things.

I could see that visits were important and beneficial, not only to the person being visited, but to the visitor. And it occurred to me that it was not only pain at seeing loved ones in this situation but the very real discomfort at not knowing what to do or what to say that kept people from visiting frequently, at length, or at all.

I wondered what could be done about it. I wondered if there was anything I could do. Over a period of months I saw that there were training sessions for employees that were extensive and thorough, but no such programs for family and friends. There were support groups, which play a critical role, but I knew from experience that rapport, relationship openness, and results-oriented work all take a long time to develop in a group. In groups, a cycle of silence and venting needs to be gone through before real work can start, and logistics usually dictate that support groups meet just once a month. Thus, a lot of time will elapse before a group moves from "soft" help to "hard" or hands-on help.

After a year or so, I came to the conclusion that visitors could benefit from something more immediate, something readily available to consult, something that could serve as a resource on the types of situations they were encountering and could anticipate encountering. I spoke to people who work with Alzheimer's patients and to people who visit family members. They felt strongly that there was a need for such a resource and encouraged me to take on the project.

This book is what resulted.

How to Use This Book

This book is not designed to be read cover to cover. It is organized in several different ways so that you can access information in the way most comfortable for you.

For example, if you want an overview of do's and don'ts, go to chapter 4. If you are looking for suggestions on how to handle uncomfortable questions and demands that are thrown at you, go to chapter 3. If there are questions you have about specific types of situations, such as how to handle repetition, how to get a conversation going, how to say "no" without creating a calamity, how to preserve everyone's dignity, how to know when to correct versus when to accept, etc., go to chapter 2.

There are also sections on how to take care of yourself, how to help your children become comfortable about visiting, and how to get started.

Chapter 1 is about the last of these. I think it is the most important part of this book. It talks about tapping into all your life experience. It talks about trusting your intuition, your common sense, your innate sense of decency, and the love and care you feel for the person you visit. When the visit is enjoyable for you, and you walk out feeling refreshed, you will know that the person you visited enjoyed the experience, too. That's what it is all about.

I would welcome suggestions and comments.

An Important Note

Though the topic is visits, and the setting is assisted living, and the focus is on people struggling with Alzheimer's disease, those words are just a convenient way to keep things simple and not muddy up the works.

The Visit

A "visit" does not have to take place away from home; it can take place *at home*. What's important is the visit itself. You can be going to visit someone; someone can be coming to visit you—this is the way we usually see a visit. But a visit can also be an interaction with a loved one who lives in the same house with you.

Most of us like visits. We look forward to them. We anticipate good food, good company, people who love us and are interested in us, conversations that are comfortable and relaxing, the sharing of interesting bits of news, the pleasure of creating an enjoyable evening for friends, or the enjoyment of going out with others to a concert, movie, dinner, sporting event, or to shop. Visits feel natural. They *include* people and make people feel included. They are warm and humanizing. When we visit, we focus on the person we are with; we each expect to enjoy the time together.

If you are caring for a loved one at home, much of your time is spent just keeping up with daily living—your needs, his needs, household chores, and the job that pays the bills. A lot of communication, or attempts at communication, take place along the way. Unfortunately, much of it is not quality communication. But if you can stop for a few minutes, several times a day, and think of your interaction as a visit, and your communication as a conversation, you will find that something special will happen. There will be a different kind of connection, and a chance for both of you to feel restored. Maybe not the first time, or even the fifth time, but with practice, and by choosing the ideas in this book that work for you, you will be able to create oases in the day for both of you.

The Setting

If that's the case, why do I talk about assisted-living environments? First of all, because this is a time in your lives when communication becomes more difficult. Secondly, because there are some special issues that arise both for the person who stays and for the person who leaves. Finally, because there hasn't been as much focus on these issues for family members as there has been for professionals.

Much of what is here will be of help, whether you are visiting with someone at home or visiting someone living in a group setting. There are different stages to this disease, and care and independent living become increasingly difficult. So once people reach the middle stages, it is often the case that they will be living in an assisted-living setting, usually a secure unit.

But don't feel locked into the concept of stages. People are very complex, and our minds are complex, too. Not only will the disease tend to attack some areas of the brain and not others, but it may not have a complete hold of those areas it is in. Plus, the brain can sometimes compensate by shifting tasks elsewhere. This means that, from moment to moment, you might find certain abilities reemerging for a time. Words, ideas, ability to understand, emotional control, all may resurface sometimes before sinking again. Sometimes people can shift several times during a single visit between earlier and later stages, and we, as visitors, need to shift with them.

Not Just Alzheimer's Disease

Problems with communication, memory, awareness, and sense of time and place can happen after a stroke, as a complication after surgery, as a symptom of Parkinson's disease, and in a number of other situations. Much of what is suggested in this book can be used in a variety of living situations: at home, in a retirement community, in assisted living, in a nursing home. And it doesn't matter how the memory problems started; much of what is suggested in this book can be helpful after stroke, after surgery, and as Parkinson's progresses.

Communication

In this book, "visiting" is not just what you do; it's how you do it. And communication is more than a transfer of information; it is the forming of a connection that includes heart and soul, thought and feeling. What transforms an interaction into a visit, and a communication into a conversation, is as simple as your state of mind.

"Visit" and "visiting" are not the only words I'd like to explain. Everyone who reads this book has a special person to visit. For some of you it's a parent, for some a grandparent; for others of you it could be a sister, a brother, a cousin, an aunt, an uncle, a friend. Sometimes the person you are visiting is male, sometimes female. So I decided to honor those differences. Sometimes I talk about his concerns or actions, sometimes about her questions or demands, sometimes about their joys and sorrows. There is no particular reason for when I chose one or the other; I've just tried to balance the amount of times I use each. The kinds of issues, experiences, and struggles that Alzheimer's disease raises do not come with a gender bias.

Chapter 1

Getting Started

Replacing Nerves with Verve

To know a little less and to understand a little more; that, it seems to me, is our greatest need.

—James Ramsey Ullman

Getting started comes down to two things. One of them, of course, is taking that first step. The other thing, which is just as important, is changing your focus. This chapter tries to answer the questions you may have about doing something you haven't done before. It points out the experience you *do* have that you can draw on, and describes some techniques you can use to make both you and your loved one comfortable.

Questions You May Have

"It's so hard to go visit. I never know what to expect. How can I prepare?"

There are so many times in life when we don't know what to expect. A boss can throw a curve ball in a meeting. A pitcher can throw a curve ball in a game. A child can ask a challenging or embarrassing question. If we relax, we can think on our feet. If we have a good answer, we provide it. If we don't, we can say we don't know. As for preparing, the best thing to do is breathe deeply, clear your mind, and go in open to whatever happens.

"How do I clear my mind?"

Just sit quietly, maybe in your car, for a minute or two before going in. It's amazing how long 60 or 120 seconds can be. It's amazing what can be accomplished in that amount of time. You can change your focus, slow your breathing, relax your muscles, change from a "get things done" mentality to a "let's see what happens" mentality.

"If the person I'm visiting asks a question I'm unprepared for, what can I say?"

It depends on the question. This is no different from other situations in life. Sometimes it's something you know, like the time or the day. Sometimes it's something you can find out, such as what's being served for dinner or how much longer until it will be served. Just offer to find out, and go do so and report back, or offer to go together to find out. Sometimes, you might have to say that you'll find out later, and let him know. This works with factual information.

But some questions may require answers he can't comprehend or doesn't want to hear. This is a judgment call, depending on how he reacted before, on how far the disease has progressed, on what kind of answer you think he expects and, most importantly, on what your own intuition tells you.

"How can I trust my intuition, when all this is so foreign to me?"

Because much of it isn't foreign to you. The place may be different, the age of the person may be different, the behavior of the particular person may be different because of Alzheimer's, but the types of questions are familiar from other contexts, and the emotions people feel are familiar from your own experience.

"What if my intuition tells me to lie?"

This is a very personal, very individual issue. There is no hard-and-fast rule, no cut-and-dried answer. Often, two things are happening simultaneously. One is happening at a thinking, or cognitive, level; the other is happening at a feeling, or emotional, level. If you can't give a truthful answer that is believable or acceptable or not hurtful at the cognitive level, then tell an emotional truth.

"How do I know what's really being asked?"

At the cognitive level, people ask questions, make specific demands, or tell you things about their lives or the people around them. For example, people ask for information, ask you to unlock a door, ask you to take them home with them, ask you what's wrong with them, ask you why they are there, ask you to call their parents to come pick them up. They may tell you they haven't had anything to eat for three days, that their parents never came to pick them up for a niece's christening, that they need to get home to cook their children's dinner.

At the emotional level, they are letting you know that they are confused, depressed, scared, frustrated, or angry, or a combination of these feelings.

"How do I offer an emotional truth?"

By acknowledging the person's feelings. Putting your arms around her and saying "how I wish I could" do whatever the specific request is. Saying to him, "It's really frustrating, isn't it?" or "You must feel so frustrated" or "Life can be really weird, sometimes," or something similar that is appropriate.

"Why is emotional truth so important?"

Because one of the hardest things for all of us is to have our fears, our concerns, our worries, dismissed. Our feelings matter. And that doesn't change as long as we are breathing. People with Alzheimer's may have trouble with mental processes, may have trouble finding the words to express the meanings in their heads, but their feelings are intact. They still bleed. They feel pain, embarrassment, joy, humor, other people's interest in them, companionship, loneliness, boredom. They can feel useful, and they can feel useless.

When someone acknowledges our feelings, the good feelings are enhanced and the bad ones are diminished.

"What if I say the wrong thing?"

This is the land of second chances. The person you are visiting won't remember what you said at the mental level. That's the silver lining of Alzheimer's and other related diseases. So it's not the words you say that are most important, and you always get another shot at them. However, emotional memory is something else. You do need to be careful about what you convey emotionally.

"What kinds of things should I be conveying on an emotional level?"

All the things you would want for yourself, all the ways you wish you could be for your children: love, sincerity, truth, respect, genuine interest, enjoyment in their company, and the sense that you like them as people.

How can you convey these things? First, you have to feel them.

You can reset your body's carburetor before walking in. There are a number of ways to do this: you can picture the needle on a speedometer going down, or your car idling in neutral because you want to listen to the end of some music; you can picture yourself on a beach with wet toes enjoying the heat of hot sand, or imagine someone rubbing your shoulders or back; you can take some deep breaths, do some isometrics, sing a favorite song.

Find what works for you. The idea is to slow things down, shut out the usual rush of things you need to do, create a space in time. People with Alzheimer's live in the moment; to convey positive emotions, you need to live in the moment, too.

What's interesting is that the better you become at creating an oasis for someone else, the more you start to feel the benefits of it yourself. As difficult as it is at first to visit, and as many challenges as continue to arise, these visits will not deplete you; instead they will become opportunities to recharge.

This may take a few months to happen, but if you focus on slowing down, living in the moment, and showing love, respect, and patience, it will happen. After a long day at work, and a mutually caring visit, you will walk out refreshed. I can make this claim because it happened to me. Just don't give up.

"What makes this approach work?"

It all comes down to dignity. Alzheimer's and related diseases threaten the dignity of sufferers, not only because of their own awareness of things not being right and of things not being in their control but also because of the way they are treated.

We can all feel if we are being patronized, condescended to, looked at strangely, ignored, talked about in front of other people as if we are not there, talked to as if we are children, ordered around. That hurts most of all. That threatens how we see ourselves.

Don't let the person become the disease. Always keep the person in your mind. By doing so, you will enhance that person's life, you will both enjoy the visits more, and you'll both want to repeat them.

Always thinking about the disease, or what could happen in a visit, or worrying about what you are going to say or do, makes it much more difficult to convey love, respect, and that you like the person. You have to walk in thinking about her, how you look forward to seeing her, how her face might light up when she sees you, or how she will make you laugh together at some incident in someone's life that she remembers. If she is likely to remind you to wear a coat because it is cold, don't get annoyed because you are an adult and she shouldn't be telling you this; take comfort in the fact that there is still someone who wants to look out for you.

If you think mostly about the disease, then the person will become the disease. You are visiting with a *person*, and both of you need to be conscious of that. You need to think it, feel it, and show it; if you are successful, you will both feel it. Not doing that threatens you, the visitor, too.

If you go because you have to, or if you are thinking about pain, anxiety, repetition, and frustration, then you'll feel much worse coming out than you did going in. Your energy will be depleted, your temperament will not stay even, and your relationship with the rest of your family could be affected. Even though you are tired, you probably won't sleep well. It will become increasingly difficult to juggle everything you need to do in your life.

There are a number of other things you can do to help yourself, and they are discussed in chapter 5.

"Are there other ways to help people keep their dignity?"

Absolutely. A key is how you deal with their sense of reality. The longer they have lived with one of these diseases, and the more advanced it is, the more important it is for *you* to accept that they have a different sense of reality, and that it's okay.

When you deny their reality, you are threatening them. You are scaring them, confusing them, frustrating them—which is not your purpose in visiting. You want to encourage positive feelings, help them have enjoyable moments in their day.

Furthermore, even if your loved ones understand everything you are saying on a mental level—and many times they won't—they are unlikely to remember it. So there's no point in putting them through it.

Again, this depends on the situation, what they can understand and what they can't, how far the disease has progressed, and what your intuition tells you. But if you decide to put them right on something, and they get upset and cling to their reality, then back off. Provide reassurance. Be prepared to say you made a mistake, or there are things you didn't know about, or that this wasn't that important after all. Then change the subject.

"How do I do that? How do I support their reality without lying?"

It isn't necessary to lie. Listen. Listen with interest. Listen and nod your head, or say "uh, huh," or "I see," every so often. Say a few things here and there that validate, not so much what they are saying but that you are listening and you care to listen to them. Listening without judging gives dignity. (This is similar to the way conveying emotional truth works: it validates both the person and his feelings.)

You can choose not to comment. This doesn't mean you agree with what has been said. It does mean you haven't "put them down" for saying it.

"Why is validation so important?"

Because having Alzheimer's doesn't mean a person is "crazy." Put yourself in his place. If you were stuck somewhere and locked in and didn't understand why and no one let you out, and there were people around you that acted decidedly strange and said things that didn't make sense—wouldn't you question your worth, your sanity, your acumen, your mental balance?

Of course you would. Maybe not immediately, but it wouldn't take too long. And that's scary. And painful. And maybe it hastens the progress of the disease. In the meantime, it drains energy to be scared and worried and sad, energy that could be used in better ways.

"What are some examples of 'denying their reality'?"

If they think their parents are still alive, that their children are still small and have to be picked up from school, or that they are going back to work tomorrow, trying to persuade them of the year, their age, and their losses would be denying their reality. Don't argue the point with them. It's not a matter of their being right or wrong. Rather, it's a matter of their believing they are in a different place and in a different time. Insisting on something else will only confuse and upset them; it won't change their perception of time and space. And if it does, it will only be momentary; they will eventually come back to their own reality. Therefore, it's much kinder (and more respectful) to listen, show you are listening, and make either sympathetic or noncommittal comments as appropriate.

Chapter 2

What to Expect

Preparing for the Possible

We live by encouragement and die without it—slowly, sadly, and angrily.

—Celeste Holm

When someone you know has Alzheimer's, a number of things can keep coming up. Here are some reasons why they occur, some suggestions on what you can do, and a glimpse of how it feels from the other side.

Repetition

Expect a lot of repetition. People struggling with Alzheimer's can't remember they just had the conversation they are now repeating. Therefore, they will say the same thing and ask the same thing over and over.

The Asking Aspect

Imagine if you couldn't remember where you were going to sleep, or who your roommate was, or even where you were. You would be very nervous, concerned, scared. When people can't remember the answer to a question, they can't stay reassured. You need to provide the reassurance over and over:

* with words

* by showing them what they need to see

* by acting as if you haven't been asked before

* by communicating in your gestures, your tone of voice, and your bearing, your complete confidence that their need will be met

Every time they ask the question, it is a new question to them. You must act as if it is a new question to you. This in itself will be reassuring to them. If you tell them they already asked you, or if you act impatient—which will let them know there is something wrong with the question—you will only be adding to their anxiety, their grief, and their fear.

What kind of questions will they ask? They'll be concerned about whether they have a room for the night, whether it's been paid for, whether anyone is sharing it with them, whether they can pay for their meal, whether someone is taking care of their house and their pets. They may need to be reintroduced to their roommate numerous times, shown where their room is over and over, have their bed pointed out, and so on.

The Telling Aspect

You will be told the same stories over and over. It could be what they did for a living, or where they live, or how they came to be where they are, or how they can't understand how they came to be there, or something about their children or their spouses or an event from the past. The content doesn't matter. What matters is that they are trying to connect through conversation. They are trying to hold on to their identities, and they are trying to hold on to their relationships, and they know that conversation is key to doing that.

They don't choose their conversational topic; it chooses them. Whatever they can draw on from memory, whatever they feel they can talk about coherently, whatever words they believe they can rely on to feel right—that's what they'll stick to as conversational fodder. These are the words they are able to find; these are the words they've been able to string together that people can follow and react to, so they hold on to them with both hands.

At the same time, they don't think they've told *you* about this before. They truly believe they are telling you about it for the first time, because they can't remember previous conversations with you. Because their working memory doesn't work very well, and because the transfer from short-term to long-term memory no longer works well either, they begin the same conversation with you every five minutes until you can succeed in changing the subject or the activity.

The best thing you can do for them is to be just as receptive, just as interested, every time the conversation repeats itself, and to not let on through words, gestures, facial expressions, tone of voice, or any other body language that you've heard it before.

Once in a while you might also say something along these lines: "I think you mentioned that once before and that is very interesting to me, because . . ." and go on to make a connection. Some possibilities are:

* "... I've done some teaching, too."

* "... my grandfather was in the navy and I love to hear about it."

* "... your wife sounds a lot like my wife."

If you are successful at getting their attention this way, the conversation may swing somewhere else for a while. But don't be surprised if it swings back.

Conversation is one of the biggest challenges visitors face, and repetition is only one facet of it. Here are some others.

Getting a Conversation Started

Greetings can be difficult. The people you visit may not be sure of who you are; you may not be sure if they remember who you are. There is no need to put it to the test. Just wade right in.

Here are some possibilities:

* "Hi, Mary. It's good to see you."

* "Hi, Joe. Did I ever have a long day! Did yours go okay?"

* "Hi. How nice to see you! Okay if I stay and talk for a while?"

* "Hi. How's it going?"

* "Hi. You look great tonight."

* "Hi. What a great color that is on you!"

* "Hi. You look so dressed up tonight. I look pretty grungy next to you."

If they question who you are, or why you are there, just give your name or say, "I came to visit you." You might add, "I hope this is a good time?" or "I enjoy spending time with you." If you give your name, just give your first name in a matter-of-fact voice. Giving your name can be tricky. You don't want to imply that they've forgotten it, or that they should have known it. But if someone says, "I don't know you," you can say, "I'm glad to meet you, my name is. . . ." This is important because, as the disease progresses, people may no longer recognize anyone who has been a part of their lives, including even their spouses and children.

Turning the Conversation

Changing the subject doesn't always work, but there are times when it is well worth trying. When people are stuck in pain or fear or anxiety or grief or frustration, directing their attention elsewhere provides some relief. This is true for everyone. But for those suffering from Alzheimer's, it can offer complete relief, even if it is only temporary. And sometimes the people who benefit most from changing the subject are the visitors.

There are a number of ways to approach changing the subject. The most effective way is to change something else first. It could be the person's physical position. If both of you are standing, propose sitting. If you are sitting, propose standing. If you are in one room, find a reason to go to another one. If you are looking in one direction, find a reason to look in another direction. Often the very change, or the reason for the change, becomes the next conversational topic.

Another way is to change the activity. If you are walking around, find a place to sit. If you are sitting, go for a walk. Stop and talk to someone else. Suggest checking out what is happening down the hall. Suggest seeing if a roommate is watching television. In the early stages, offer a choice of activities. For example, "Would you like to take a walk or play bingo?" Later on, however, it's better to ask one thing at a time. If the walk is rejected, *then* suggest bingo.

A third way is to introduce another topic of conversation. It could be related to what is being discussed. It could be about something similar that has happened to you. It could be a compliment on her clothing or a request for advice.

Another possibility is talking about how tired you are because of a long day at work and how you'd like to just sit quietly together and rest your eyes, and would that be all right with him? Then thank him for helping you.

Ending a Conversation

Leaving is a challenge, too. It's amazing how talkative some people will become to delay your departure, and how smoothly they'll avoid acknowledging your cues that you need to go. Even though it's really not the same, it can feel similar to dealing with a child who just can't manage to get to bed, can't manage to turn out the light, can't manage to stop calling out one last comment, one last request. Remember, these are adults who feel lost, lonely, and abandoned. They are trying to hold on to their connection with you.

Remind them how much you've enjoyed the visit. Tell them you'll be back soon. Ask them if you can come and visit again. You can say:

* "I enjoyed this so much."

* "I always feel good after talking to you."

* "Seeing you is the best part of my day."

* "I don't think I laughed this much all day; thanks so much."

* "I want to come again; is that okay with you?"

* "Would it be okay if I come and visit again?"

* "This was great."

* "It's so much fun talking to you. You tell great stories."

* "You are so feisty. I should be taking lessons from you."

* "I'd like to come back in a couple of days. Will it be okay if I stop by?"

Tell them you need to go: to get to work, to do homework, to have dinner.

* "I didn't realize how late it was. No wonder my stomach is growling. I didn't have dinner yet."

* "I'd better go before you hear my stomach rumble."

* "I need to cook dinner tonight and I still need to get the groceries! I guess I'd better get moving."

* "I forgot to have dinner and it's way past time. I'd better go before I fall over on you."

* "I'd really better go. I've lots of paperwork to do yet tonight."

* "I need to get going. I'm supposed to get to work early tomorrow."

If your leaving is traumatic, have a staff member help you. Once the person you care about it engaged in something else, you can slip out quietly. This is not the best approach to leaving, but it is better than having someone hang on to you in tears, or fight to get through a door as you try to close it.

Other Conversation Considerations

Where Questions Can Help and Where They Can Hurt

Questions are tricky. Generally, it is better to ask *close-ended* questions than open-ended questions. Close-ended questions can be answered with "yes" or "no" or "maybe" or "I don't know" or "I don't remember." Here are some examples of close-ended questions that are pretty safe:

* "Do you like to watch television?"

* "Would you like to watch television?"

* "Would you like to go on a walk with me?"

* "Does it taste good?"

* "Is it okay if I stay and visit with you?"

* "Do you feel warm enough today?"

* "Have we met before?"

* "Do you two know each other?"

The key is to ask questions that people can answer with a "yes" or a "no" and to avoid questions that might lead to an "I don't know" or an "I don't remember." Don't ask questions that might be on a quiz show. Don't ask questions that require retrieving information from memory. Don't ask questions about the past—and, depending on the person you are visiting, that can include things that happened five minutes ago.

Questions to avoid include asking if they had lunch, if they got their hair done, if their clothes are new. When they realize that they don't know how to answer the question, it's demoralizing. The best thing for you to do is to *not* put them in that position, and the best way to do that is to only ask questions about what is happening right now and what they are feeling right now.

Open-ended questions require more of an answer. In most situations, it is open-ended questions that get a conversation going. But much of the time this is very tricky to do with people who suffer from Alzheimer's and related conditions. Here are some examples of open-ended questions and demands you would want to *avoid*:

* "What television programs do you like to watch?"

* "What do you like to do?"

* "Tell me a story from when you were little."

* "What are your favorite foods?"

These are *not* good questions to ask because the other person has to be able to remember two things—the answer and the words to communicate the answer. He might be able to visualize a show

he liked, she might remember the taste of a wonderful meal, but that doesn't mean either of them
can remember the name for these things. So what
seems like a simple question is actually a pretty
complex memory challenge.

Some open-ended questions can work though,
such as:

* "How did your day go?"

* "How are you?"

These work because we have polite answers
we've learned to say that don't necessarily repre-
sent how we feel, but that we have the habit of
answering in a certain way. These questions and
answers are somewhat automatic. They are a sort of
conversational lubricant—they grease the skids in
conversations between people whose relationship is
superficial, or between people who are just
exchanging a few words in passing. Because of this,
these questions are relatively easy to field and don't
require searching our memory banks.

Sometimes an open-ended question can work
if combined with an opportunity to say "no." For
example, the request "tell me a story from when
you were little," which could put someone on the
spot, could be phrased another way:

* "I'd love to hear a story from when you were little. Do you feel like telling one now?"

* "Is this a good time to tell me a story?"

By asking it this way, no one is put on the spot, but the door is open for reminiscing.

How to handle using questions in conversations will depend on the individual's personality, conversational style, and current verbal abilities. Sadly, the longer people contend with Alzheimer's, the more they lose verbal skills. While open-ended questions may work in the early stages, and close-ended ones in the middle stages, eventually—and with some people sooner rather than later—questions will be a source of confusion, frustration, and pain.

That's why it is important for all of us to be aware of how much we depend on questions in our culture. It is almost automatic in our society to get a conversation started and to keep it going by using questions. But questions force responses, and just the sound of a question can put a person on the spot. If she can't remember the answer, or doesn't understand the question, she knows she isn't fulfilling an expectation. And even though she no longer understand the words, she still can recognize that a question is being asked.

Try watching a television program or movie in a language you don't know. You will be able to tell from the tone and pitch of the voice, from the facial expressions and the body language, when a question is being asked. You will also be able to tell mood—joy, pleasure, anger, sadness, energy, fatigue, patience, frustration, tension, calm. People with Alzheimer's can read your tone, even when they can't grasp the content of your words.

When You Can't Understand What They Are Saying

Sometimes people will start sentences but not be able to finish them. They will try starting a sentence several times. It might start off with "I want you to . . ." and then end with garbled words, or words that don't make sense, or just sounds of frustration. Other times, the entire communication is garbled and you can't make sense of it.

One approach is just to acknowledge what is happening: "It's frustrating, isn't it? You can't find the words you want and I'm having trouble guessing what you mean. I'm sorry." Showing understanding of the situation, your part in it, and your empathy are all a form of respect. I've seen people smile the most wonderful smiles and relax their bodies after I say this. Saying this shows that you know their thoughts are still working, that you know they are still in there even though they can't communicate effectively. They recognize that you are talking to them as one adult to another. This is an enormous relief to them, and it helps them hold on to who they are.

Then, if you have the time and the inclination, you can try something else. You can ask them if they'd like you to try guessing a few possibilities. If they are interested in trying, explain that they'd just have to answer "yes" or "no" or "you're getting close" or something like that as you pose questions. If they understand this and want to go ahead, try going through a sequence. Start by asking about categories:

* "Does it have to do with food?"

* "Does it have to do with your room?"

* "Does it have to do with clothing?"

* "Does it have to do with sleep?"

* "Does it have to do with another person?"

* "Does it have to do with me somehow?"

* "Does it have to do with going somewhere?"

* "Does it have to do with getting something?"

* "Does it have to do with doing something?"

If you can narrow it down to a category, then you can work within the category. If it's one of the last three, maybe they can show you. If it's about food, you can then ask whether they're hungry, or if there is a particular food they would like to have. And you can just keep on narrowing it down. *But be careful not to do this for more than a minute or so*, because if they forget the original reason for the questions, they will have a new reason to be frustrated.

Pay attention to body language. If the person you are talking to is fidgeting, he might need to use the bathroom. If he is grabbing at you, he might need a hug. Her facial expression may indicate that she is in pain; ask if she can point to where it hurts.

The third approach is to check with staff members. They might be aware of something that has come up before—when maybe the words *were* accessible from memory.

If it all gets too difficult, you can follow the first approach with a hug and express the hope that the two of you can figure it out later. Then suggest doing something else in the meantime. For example, say: "In the meantime, why don't we go for a walk?"

Lastly, you can shake your head regretfully and say you don't know anything about that, that you wish you could help, but you were just on your way somewhere. Then repeat that you're sorry you can't help, say you'll visit another time, and move on.

Ways to Say "No"

Sometimes you have to say "no," but there are a variety of ways to say it:

* "I wish I could."

* "Oh, that would be nice."

* "If only we could."

* "I don't know. I'll see what I can find out."

* "I wonder who I should see to find out?"

* "What a great idea. Maybe we could plan something."

* "That's an idea, but this isn't a good time."

* "Could we talk about it next time I come?"

* "Are you sure? I'll see what I can do."

* "I think it's too cold today."

* "I think it's too hot today."

* "Did you notice it's pouring out today? How about we try it another time?"

* "Is that something you love to do? I never knew that."

* "It sure sounds like fun."

* "Maybe there's a mix-up about the day (or time)?"

These are the best approaches. Sometimes they don't work. A last-ditch approach is to pass the buck, but it is best to use that approach *only* when it is appropriate, and it is only appropriate in certain situations.

What situations are those? Generally, when you are asked something you cannot decide, do not know, or should not do. Some requests can only be answered by a staff member. If people think you are a staff member, they will ask permission for things you can't provide or don't want to provide. If you consistently give them cues that you are not a staff member, then when they make such a request, you can say you are not a staff member and they'll believe you.

This makes boundaries important. Make a point of saying you are visiting, that you are glad you are visiting, how much you enjoy the visit, and so on. When something comes up that is clearly a staff decision, you'll be able to say regretfully that you don't work there. That you are just there to visit them. They'll understand that you don't have control over everything, either.

Ways to Indicate You Are Listening

* "How interesting!"

* "Sounds like a plan."

* "I see."

* "Really?"

* "I didn't know about that."

* "You never told me that before."

* "Thanks for telling me."

* "Well, *that's* something."

* "I'd heard that."

* "I see what you mean."

* "Is *that* right?"

* "Is *that* so?

* "*Did* it?

* "Okay."

* "How nice."

* "Sounds nice."

* "Sounds good."

Even if all you can say is "uh, huh" or "oh," they will know you are listening.

Ways to Encourage Action

Often the idea that something might be fun for them to do will not move people at all. However, if you indicate it would be enjoyable for you, they may well decide it's worth doing. This may be because the decision is being left in their hands. It may also be because it is an opportunity for them to do the giving instead of the receiving, for them to be independent instead of dependent. Here are some examples of things that can be said:

* "I'm looking forward to doing it. Would you like to come along?

* "I'd enjoy it more if you kept me company."

* "I'm heading there now; will you walk with me?

* "I'm going to give it a shot; want to watch me?"

* "A hot shower is one of my favorite things. I don't mind waiting while you enjoy yours. I'll just sit here and snooze while you're gone."

* "I'd hate for you to miss it. Can I come along?"

* "I'd hate for you to miss it. I'll just wait here for you until you're done, and then we'll go."

* "I'm pretty hungry. Would you mind if I joined you?"

* "It's great to do things together."

When to Insist, When Not to Insist

Unless it is a matter of physical safety, there is little reason to insist on anything. Encourage them to eat, sleep, walk, join in activities, yes. But insist? No. Many things are not a matter of life and death to the body. But they can feel to people like a matter of life and death to the soul. There are very few things that they can control, very few areas in which they feel any measure of independence. Where decision-making can be left to them, make sure they can keep it. Instead of seeing their resistance to something you want them to do as a personal affront to you, or as a foolish whim on their part, look at it as an opportunity for them to make decisions, to feel autonomous, to feel they are respected. What could be better for them!

This is not easy. Don't think of them as your two-year-old who is testing his use of the word "no" and his ability to stand up to you and your ability to bend. They passed two a long time ago. It may feel the same to you, but it is not the same to them. They are giving you the opportunity to show them you respect their wishes, you respect their right to make decisions, and you love the essence of who they are. Be glad of the opportunity.

Interacting with Others

The hallway along which your loved one lives is his neighborhood. In normal social situations, when we walk past our neighbors, we nod our heads in passing or stop to say hello. If we are new to the neighborhood, we stop and introduce ourselves. If we are visiting someone else, and encounter *his* neighbors, he introduces us.

It's important to recreate this normalcy as much as possible. The person you are visiting isn't likely to remember names, and may not remember meeting the people along his hallway.

That means it's up to you. If you walk together, make a point of stopping where someone else is standing or sitting and making the introductions yourself. It doesn't matter that the others won't remember it several moments later. The interaction will be familiar and seem normal to both of them; they will enjoy the content while it takes place and perhaps enjoy the emotional memory of it later.

Simple, ordinary conversation will suffice:

* "Hi. Have you two met? Do you two know each other?"

* "This is Joe. I'm Sara. What's your name?"

* "It's nice to meet you, Mary. Joe, this is Mary. Mary, this is Joe."

You can talk about the fact you are on a walk, or that Joe hasn't been here long, or compliment Mary on something she is wearing, or just say you look forward to seeing her again, that you enjoyed talking to her.

You might repeat this on many visits. Eventually, they'll know they know each other even if they don't know each other's names. If they don't, it doesn't matter. The important thing is making each visit as much like normal social interaction as possible.

Besides, introducing and reintroducing happens in normal social interaction, too. Do you remember everyone you've met? Or even that you met them before?

Interacting with Staff and Management

Staff members are your allies and your partners. When both you and they keep that in mind things go more smoothly.

Staff members can answer questions, help with tricky situations, be firm when you want to be the lenient one. However, you need to recognize that the staff is there all day, and staff members not only have a different perspective—which includes playing all the roles of parent—but they have to pace themselves during the course of a long day, balance the needs of many people, and accomplish many tasks that are a part of their job, leaving them little time for one-on-one interaction.

Often, staff members are tired, frustrated, and burned out. Usually, they are underpaid and have a second or third job in addition to this one. Many want to spend more time in walking, talking, and giving positive strokes to the people in their care, but they have to serve so many meals, do so many laundries, handle so many hygiene and personal care issues, dispense so many medications, organize so many group activities, that it is difficult to find time for the one-on-one interactions that drew them to their job in the first place.

You, the visitor, come in with pain. You come for a part of the day, and you come with your attention focused on one person. However, like the staff members, you often come in tired, frustrated, and burned out.

In many ways, staff and family members have a lot in common. When they work together, they need to keep that in mind. When staff members approach family members, they need to think of the family members' pain and feeling of powerlessness to help someone they love. When family members approach staff members, they need to think of the many demands placed on *them*, and the pain they must feel knowing that they, too, are helpless to stop the progress of the disease.

Staff members are individuals, as well. They have different amounts of training, different skills, different experiences from each other. Some are very young. They also have different personalities and different abilities when it comes to dealing with stress. Some are more verbal and can think of the right things to say at the right time. Some are better with smiles and touch. Some have more patience than others. Just like the rest of us.

Always treat staff members with respect and assume that they will do the best they can. It is always possible to escalate. It is difficult to retreat.

Consider asking their opinion about something. Consider asking how you can work together. And consider asking how *you* can help.

If there is something you disagree with, don't come at them with both barrels. Don't start out by telling them they're wrong, by giving them orders, by complaining, or by getting angry.

Instead, ask about the situation or the approach. Tell them you're confused by what happened. Sometimes they will not have seen what you saw. Sometimes they will have an interesting—and acceptable—reason for their approach. Give them a chance to tell you. Give yourself a chance to consider their perspective. You may find it valid.

In any case, most people, if approached in a reasonable way and with an open mind, will be prepared to reciprocate. That means they'll be interested in how you saw it and in what your concerns are and, maybe, in the approach you'd prefer to see. No matter what they say, thank them for explaining their views and acknowledge what they are trying to do.

Of course, it's important to avoid approaching them all the time. It's a little like the story about the boy who cried wolf: if they get the idea that they can see you coming, they won't be able to hear what you say.

Don't think of them as your employees. Think of them as your partners. Make sure they can feel your respect for them as people and as caretakers. They deserve it. Your loved one deserves it.

What if you can't resolve a problem? You might have to go to the next level of management. Try to find a solution that works for everyone, while always keeping in mind that the people at the heart of the situation cannot speak for themselves. In some fashion, everyone involved should be speaking for them. The staff knows that, too.

When They're Talked about as If They Weren't There

It's a horrible feeling to be talked about as if one isn't there, and it happens to people in secure units all the time. It makes them feel invisible—as if they are being erased. It is embarrassing, humiliating, degrading, demeaning.

It happens all the time; it happens without thinking. Visitors do it; staff members do it. They talk with each other about someone's life history, medical history, lack of memory, and they talk about their own frustrations. They talk about what someone just did: how he acted, how they can't understand her, or how they have to go clean him up or change her because of an accident. Sometimes weaknesses, accidents, failings, and anger are put in very graphic language.

It's important to keep on your toes and avoid doing this yourself. You may think it doesn't make a difference because some of it your loved one might not understand and all of it will be forgotten. But it does make a difference. The feeling of being treated that way will remain.

If you have things you need to say to someone about the person you are visiting, find a way to talk out of earshot. If others start making inappropriate comments in front of him, interrupt them gently and ask if you can talk to them for a couple of minutes. Then walk away with them to another room, or down the hall. Remember the adult you are visiting, and keep extending the same courtesies you would to other adults in any other social situations. Don't forget to excuse yourself before you walk off with someone else.

Touch

When to touch? When not to touch? It's simple. Ask.

* "I'm really in the mood for a hug. What about you?"

* "I could really use a hug. Any chance you could give me one?"

* "I'd love a hug."

* "Would you mind if I kissed you on the cheek before I go?"

Let them decide. Let them know that *they* are giving *you* something. And make sure to thank them:

* "That felt great. Thanks."

* "Can we do that again, sometime?"

* "Can I have another hug? How about right now?"

They may take the initiative. Sometimes they will ask. Sometimes they will just reach out. They might take your hand, or lean on you, or pat you on the shoulder, head, or back. They might take your arm or put an arm around your waist. Just handle it naturally. It's a compliment to your love and your sincerity. It's evidence of trust.

There's a reassurance and a comfort that comes from touch. It is like nothing else.

Sometimes communicating with words just doesn't work. If they can't understand your question, try showing them. Touch your own face, then touch theirs. Give yourself a hug first. Smile; make appreciative sounds. Then reach out toward them and watch their body language. If it is open, leaning, smiling, relaxed—then gently put your arms on their shoulders, and if they seem comfortable, then give them a hug. And express your pleasure at receiving one.

Other Forms of Touch

Some people like hand massages. Others like their hair stroked. And some prefer other sensory experiences, such as sounds, aromas, and flavors. Bring flowers and music. Try a dance video. Or try other types of stimulation. Something slippery, something soft, something warm, something textured.

Touch can mean love. Try bringing a stuffed animal. A blanket. A doll. A pillow. One of the best things to bring is an animal. Petting a dog or cat helps people feel connected.

Fierce and Painful Emotions

Unfortunately, there are many. This section describes some of the most common ones.

Sense of Betrayal

Many people feel an acute sense of betrayal, especially in the first weeks after moving into a secure unit. This is normal. They find themselves in a strange place with staff people who direct what they can do or not do, with neighbors who seem strange and sick, and with doors that never open out for them.

They are locked in a place they can't leave, they don't know their way around, everyone around them is strange, and the only room they can call their own resembles a motel room and is shared with a stranger. Most of their possessions have gone missing, too. And how did they get there? The people they loved and trusted put them there.

This is scary. It makes them angry, it makes them sad, it makes them afraid. And when their loved ones come to visit them, they can smell their visitors' fear, resentment, grief, and guilt—and that makes them feel even more betrayed.

Wouldn't you feel that way, too?

Some people fall into a depression. Others get angry and keep rushing the door that is locked. Some try to seduce visitors who are strangers to them into opening the door for them. They do this by putting on a coat, carrying a pocketbook, and weaving a perfectly normal-sounding conversation.

It is important to respect their feeling of betrayal. It is an honest emotion and an honest reaction. Don't belittle it. Don't dismiss it. Instead, accept it. Acknowledge it. Show that you've never stopped caring.

What's hard is that we, as visitors, feel even more guilty when we are faced with their feelings of betrayal. It forces us to face the fact that they are still the people they were; that they know that control over their lives has been wrested from them; that they know they are in a strange place; and that they know that their loved ones did this.

To them this new place is a prison. The boredom and sameness of each hour of each day is torture. There is emptiness. The comfort of familiar surroundings, familiar routines, familiar objects, has all disappeared.

They feel impotent. So do we. We need to convey that, though we are powerless to give them back the life they had, our power to love them will never be diminished.

What If You Were Not Involved in Placing Them There?

If you are visiting a friend, you can validate his feelings. Here are some things you may want to say:

* "I'm so sorry this happened."

* "How hard it must be."

* "It must be a terrible feeling."

* "I don't blame you for feeling this way."

* "I can't blame you for feeling this way."

You can change the direction of the conversation.

* "Tell me about your house."

* "Tell me about where you lived before."

* "Was it a lot of work?"

* "It sounds nice."

You can offer reassurance.

* "I'll find out about your pets."

* "I'm sure your neighbors must be caring for them."

* "It sounds like you took good care of everything."

* "It's so nice to see people have pride in things."

You can make positive suggestions:

* "Have you been sick lately? Have some things become difficult to do? Maybe you need to concentrate on getting your strength back."

* "Well, eating properly and going for walks might help. I should be doing more of that myself. But I've not been very good about it. If I

made myself take a walk, would you keep me company?"

You can provide a silver lining:

* "There's one good thing; it's given me the opportunity to meet you, and I'm glad to have met you."

What If You Are the One Who Made This Painful Decision?

Remind him that you love him. Reassure her that you are always seeking the best for her. Promise that you will always be there.

Don't make excuses. Don't try to justify what you've done. These are arguments that can't be won because there are no good answers. The conversation will only become more painful; it will end in anger and in tears, and there will be no resolution or healing.

Stick to emotional truths. Stick to validation. You can't agree to take him home. You can't agree to her caring for herself. You can't agree to home care if you can't afford it. You can't agree that you had other options if there really weren't any. But you can agree with his or her feelings. You can agree that this is not as nice as home. You can agree that it feels rotten not to have a choice. You can agree you'd be angry, too. You can agree that life sometimes stinks.

And then the two of you can hug and cry and find something to laugh about, preferably something patently silly.

Most important, you can continue to come. It takes a lot of strength to visit when you know you'll be greeted with anger, when you know the person you love might call you names and say he hates you. It takes strength to realize that this is normal, and that if you keep coming, and handle the anger without lashing out, that the anger will eventually decrease. When you give your loved one the chance to express the anger, by continuing to come and listen, you are proving to him that he is not being deserted.

Try not to overinterpret. Don't assume. People can be angry for different reasons. Most people are uncomfortable with change; some people fear change. The anger may have less to do with you than it has to do with things being different. Or there may be fear about what may happen next; if things changed once, they could again. That's scary, especially if someone doesn't see it coming, and especially if he has no control over it. Fear often underlies anger. If you can remember that, you'll be able to handle the anger washing over you with relative tranquility, and you'll be able to react with compassion.

Embarrassment and Humiliation

Not remembering. Spilling food. Having spots on clothes. Seeing someone else be chastised. Having a staff member insist on a shower right now even though a visitor is there. Being told to go to bed in front of someone else. Hearing toilet accidents announced publicly. Being denied simple requests. Being treated as invisible.

These are humiliating things. They make clear that she isn't considered an adult anymore. That he isn't worthy of respect. That she isn't seen as having dignity.

If we do nothing else, we must work to preserve our loved ones' dignity. We must make sure they know that we respect them, we admire them, we love them.

We must make sure we never call their attention to memory lapses or food spills. We must make sure we never humiliate them in any way.

And we must consider how to handle situations when we see them humiliated.

One option is to point it out privately to the staff member, afterwards. This is tricky. It must be done gently and tactfully, or it will be taken the wrong way. You might want to say:

* "I wonder if there'd be another way to do that? I'm not sure why, but that didn't feel too comfortable for me hearing it, so I imagine it wasn't too comfortable for you, either? What do you think?"

Meanwhile, give your loved one a hug to acknowledge the pain of it, and show your disapproval. By doing this, you help to restore his self-respect. By doing this you show that you would never speak that way and that you respect him as much as you always did. You might say something like this:

* "That was really odd. Are you okay?"

* "I'm sorry that happened."

* "That wasn't right. I'm really surprised by it."

* "Are you okay? I sure wouldn't have liked that."

* "That person must be having a bad day. That wasn't appropriate."

* "That person must be having a bad day. I don't remember seeing her act that way before."

* "I wonder what got into her today?"

* "That was uncomfortable, wasn't it?"

Or, you may simply use body language:

* Shrug your shoulders.

* Shake your head.

* Roll your eyes.

Sometimes the staff member may think he is being helpful, or may be doing what he has been trained to do. For example, he may automatically cut someone's food into bite-sized pieces at the table, or lay out her clothes for the day. However, if she is used to cutting her own food, she gets the message that she is not seen as capable, that she is seen as a child or incompetent, and that she is being treated accordingly. This can make her feel useless. And not being able to choose what she will wear each day has the same effect, plus it makes her feel as if nothing is within her control.

What can you say if someone you are visiting complains about these things? You can use a combination of humor, validation, and an offer of help:

* "It sounds like you're getting the royal treatment. You know, like in the movies, when people have a private maid or valet to lay out their clothes and tie their ties."

* "I guess some special treatment once in a while can't hurt."

* "I'll see what I can do. It might be nice to have someone do that for me once in a while, but I'm not sure I'd like it all the time, either."

You can talk to a staff member about it privately and tactfully. You can mention that she's been used to cutting her food and choosing her clothes and, as far as you know, is still capable of it. Explain that you are concerned because she has mentioned it to you and made a point of saying she wants to do it herself and feels useless because she doesn't have the chance to do even that much for herself. Ask if there would be a problem with her having a knife for a short time during a meal. Ask if it would be possible for her to describe the clothes she wants to wear if she isn't steady enough on her feet to get them out of the closet herself.

Little things like this can help with self-confidence, with mental health, with staying engaged with life. The more people can do for themselves, the better off they will be and the slower will be their decline. Staying active, in these small ways, generates self-respect and sustains personal dignity. Making small decisions, taking action rather than being acted upon, gives both purpose and pleasure to the moments in their day. All of these together make life worth living.

How they perceive themselves can affect their health. This is true for all of us.

Here's one more example of how something simple can make a difference. Some people like to wear shirts and blouses tucked in; some people like to wear them out. If your friend's personal style has always been one way, and a staff person begins to dress him the other way, he will feel different. He might not be able to express it, but he will resent it. To him, this is not who he is. What hurts is that he is not being seen for who he is by the staff person, and now other people won't see him for who he is, either. What scares him is that he is losing control over who he is, and maybe he will lose that control in all kinds of ways.

The staff person isn't doing anything wrong. It's simply a matter of not knowing the habits or preferences of those being helped. However, if the person you are visiting comments on it to you, or you notice for yourself that his personal style has changed, you can quietly check with the staff to see if he had expressed a desire to change it. By asking the question, you alert the staff to the change and to the realization that here is something they weren't aware of. Often, people will be glad to know.

Grief, Pain, and Fear

Dementia affects people in different ways. Some people react by crying all the time. It's not clear how much this is within their control. There are a variety of ways to handle this.

* Hug them and tell them you care.

* Give them a smile hello.

* Hold out a hand and ask if they'd like to walk for a while.

* Hold out a hand and say, "Let's walk for a while," and then just start doing it.

* Start talking to them about something else.

* Compliment them on something they are wearing.

* Just greet them and tell them what a beautiful day it is.

However, the crying might not be a part of the dementia; it might be a reaction to it. Grieving at the loss of their regular life is to be expected. We would cry, too, at the prospect of everything continuing to be less, at so many losses in bodily function, mental function, relationships, everyday activities, possessions, and familiar surroundings.

Sometimes, when we move, it seems as if all our ties are severed. Ties to family are cut, ties to friends are cut, ties to community are cut, ties to memories are cut, ties to the past are cut. This kind of grief is easier for us to respond to because it is familiar. It makes sense. This kind of grief is about how age and illness betray us. Hugs, shared sorrow, acknowledgment, taking each day as it comes—the usual approaches to grief—are what you can offer. They may not seem to help all the time, but if nothing else, your effort helps.

Grief can turn into depression. It's not uncommon and it's not surprising. These are a lot of negative life changes at once: loss of home, loss of possessions, loss of decision-making power; fear of losing things, fear of loss of memory, fear of not being sure who they are or who you are; fear of being alone; fear of not knowing where to go or what to do or where they are supposed to be; fear of not having a place to stay; fear of not knowing how to get home. Depression can be helped with therapy; depression can be helped with medication. However, the causes of the depression are real; they will not go away; and the prospects for something better someday if we wait long enough, pray long enough, live long enough, aren't there, either. So some of the approaches, some of the things you would say to a person in the outside world, would be lies here.

Helping people who are diagnosed as clinically depressed requires professional help. Helping people with other forms of depression is different. Help them with their grief and help them to live in the moment—no looking forward, no looking back. Eventually, this is a place that people suffering from Alzheimer's will reach anyway. In the meantime, helping them live in the moment, and helping them make those moments purposeful and pleasurable, will chip away at the depression.

Jealousy and Envy

The person you visit could be jealous if you spend time talking to other people.

Also, if you visit a lot, the other people may become envious of the person you visit.

Both of these work out and dissipate over time, as long as the person you visit is made to feel secure that she is still the primary focus of your visit, and as long as the others get a little of your time and the full focus of your attention during those moments.

Romance

The need for connection, the need for relationships, does not go away. For some people, a romantic relationship is more energizing, more validating, more reassuring, than almost anything else. It is not uncommon to see men and women flirting, holding hands, walking arm in arm, walking with an arm around each other's waist. There is joy on their faces, a lilt in their voice, a jaunt to their step. It gives them happiness, it gives them a sense of purpose, of being wanted, of being valued, of connectedness, of sharing. It fills emotional needs that are not being filled elsewhere.

It doesn't usually progress beyond flirtation and friendship, but sometimes it does. Sometimes they'll stop to hug and kiss. Sometimes they'll be found cuddling in their rooms. This can be uncomfortable for adult children to watch. It can be uncomfortable for a spouse who is no longer recognized or remembered.

But it does no harm to the people engaging in it. It adds color and meaning to their lives. Doctors have a special rule to follow: "First, do no harm." What family members need to think about is that, as independent adults, these loved ones had the discretion, the right, the independence, to enter into relationships. Though suffering certain impairments, they are still adults, these are activities they remember with pleasure, these are activities that still give them pleasure.

If loved ones still have romantic needs and sexual urges, and it won't harm anyone, let them be. Their world is getting smaller and smaller, their memories fewer and fewer, their activity less and less. Hard as it is, we all need to remember that we are not their parents, and only interfere where their safety is an issue.

Chapter 3

How to Respond

An Ear Is Worth a Thousand Tongues

*Though one can't always
Remember exactly why one has been happy,
There is no forgetting that one was.*

—W. H. Auden

75

When you visit someone with Alzheimer's or a related condition, it is likely that you will interact with other people, too. Any of these people may ask you questions or make requests. They may plead with you to do something. Many times such requests will come from the loved one who shares your home. There are no perfect answers, but here are some responses you could try.

Things They May Ask or Say

"Please take me home with you."

This is heartbreaking. The only answer is to put your arms around them and say "how I wish I could," or something like it, in as heartfelt a tone as you can.

One of the ways to avoid having people ask you to take them home is to avoid giving them signals that you will be able to leave. For example, wearing a coat or jacket shows you came from outside and will be leaving. Carrying a handbag or a backpack indicates you have freedom of movement, too. If you will be entering a secure unit, lock whatever you are carrying in the car and hang your coat up in a lobby closet. And keep your keys out of sight, too.

Depending on the situation, you might want to avoid mentioning that you came by car. Many people in secure units are looking for a way out, and they know transportation is a key to accomplishing that. Raising their hopes, even though you don't do it purposely, is cruel.

Alternatively, again depending on the situation, you might want to say that taking them with you just isn't possible today because you have to get to work, or you have an appointment to get to. But this isn't the best approach, because it underscores the fact that you are able to leave, and there are times you might not be able to say it because it wouldn't be true. You need to be sincere, so they can perceive you as sincere. That sincerity will be comforting to them. It is very important to feel the sincerity of the people around us when our whole world seems to have been turned upside down.

"I want to call my parents so they can pick me up."

In most cases, people who have reached the age to suffer from Alzheimer's or a related disease no longer have parents who are living. What good would it do to tell them their parents have died and make them suffer the shock of grief and loss all over again? Instead, there are a number of ways to handle this.

Some involve focusing the conversation on their parents. You could say:

* "Your parents really loved you, didn't they?"

* "Tell me about them."

* "I'll bet your father was tall, like you."

Other responses involve appealing to reason, which often works. You might refer to the weather: "It's really cold (or rainy) outside, why not wait for tomorrow? I don't think you'd want them to come out in this weather." Or, if it is starting to get dark, you might refer to it being nicer to travel in the daytime.

Sometimes this means asking questions. Usually, you want to avoid asking the kind of questions that might make them realize they can't remember the answers. In this case, though, you want them to realize that they can't. For example, if they insist on calling, agree that calling is always a good idea, and ask if they have a phone. Ask if they have the telephone number handy. Chances are they won't.

You can also refer to the waste of money that leaving now would entail: "I don't know, it seems silly to throw all that money away." Pause. "Well, I think your dinner is paid for, and a room for the night, too. Why not take advantage of it? It's all paid for after all, and then you can see about things, tomorrow."

"Let's just go. You can drive me there, right?"

Don't get into the issue of whether you have a car or not. It could involve lying, and it wouldn't be too believable anyway. Instead, tell them you're not sure of the address and how to get there, and ask if they have all that information somewhere.

If they do, ask if they have a key to the place. If they don't, explain that you'd hate to take them there and find that they couldn't get in. Explain that it's always better to be expected. Offer to try another time.

"Where's the way out of here? Is that the door? Can you unlock it?"

These are tough questions. It's clear that you came in somehow, and that you'll be leaving somehow, too. How you handle this will depend on personality, the progress of the disease, and your comfort level. If the person is very confused, you can suggest walking in a certain direction to check, and then try to turn the conversation before you get there. You might ask where they are planning to go and how they are planning to get there. If it is true, you could say that public transportation isn't running, or isn't available. And suggest trying the next day. In some situations, if they are in the early stages of the disease, you might be able to remind them of what they are struggling with, and explain that, for now, this is the best place to be to learn to cope with it. You might want to consult with a caregiver before taking that approach, however. If it is not something they can absorb or handle, you might simply say that they aren't feeling well right now and they have to work on getting better.

If they are very direct and point to the correct door to the outside, you could verify it, but add that you don't have a key to it. You could say that this isn't the right time for it to be open. Suggest that the two of you do something else in the meantime.

"I need to talk to someone in charge. Where's the office?"

Usually there is a nurse's office within the secure unit and an administrative office outside. You can direct people to the nurse's office. This can be helpful because if they want something that the nurses can't or shouldn't provide, the nurses should have a protocol they can follow.

However, sometimes it is the administrative office that is wanted. If you are visiting on a weekend, you can say that the office is probably closed because it is the weekend, but that they could certainly check on Monday.

"Do I know you?"

If a relative or someone you have known a long time asks you this, tell the truth. Say, "Yes, but we haven't seen each other for a while." If you've changed anything about your appearance—such has hair length, style, or color; your weight; your glasses; your clothing style, size, or colors—or if your voice has changed in some way, becoming hoarser, deeper, higher, breathier; or if you've been sick so that you are much paler, then point out the change and comment on how your friends have been doing double takes.

If you've only just met, or have met only a few times, because this person happens to live where the person you visit lives, then try one of the following approaches:

* "No, we haven't really met before, but it's really nice to meet you."

* "We only met once, very briefly, but we didn't get a chance to talk. It's nice to have a chance to do that now."

* "I'm not sure if we have met. You look familiar, but I can't remember meeting you. I'm happy to meet you now, though."

"Who are you?"

If someone you've known long and well asks you this, just give your name. Say you're a friend of, or a son of, so-and-so's, and "I'd like to visit, if it's a good time for you?" This puts the emphasis on spending time together, and also puts control of the visit in the other person's hands. You don't want them to dwell on not being able to recognize someone, which is painful and embarrassing. When the visit is over, state how much you've enjoyed the visit and how you'd like to come again, if that's okay. Put a slight question in your voice. When you are invited to come back, say "thank you" warmly, and say you'll come soon. Then leave.

"I'm so tired. I want to sleep."

You can offer to walk them to their room and help them lie down for a rest. Or you could suggest going for something to drink or a bite to eat. This depends on their diet, and their caregiver's feelings about snacks. Often, when someone is tired, a glass of juice, a bowl of ice cream, or a can of nutritional supplement can be reviving. The combination of fluids, sugar, and the feeling of being given a special treat boost both physical and emotional energy. This is particularly true in the middle and later stages of the disease, when people lose interest in food, and refuse to eat at mealtime and become dehydrated.

However, it is important to always check with a nurse first. Some people are diabetic and can't have sugar. Others are on restricted diets for other reasons. Liquid food is usually prescribed by a doctor. If you know your loved one gets a can of liquid food every evening to supplement her diet, you will still have to check to make sure she hasn't already had her drink that evening.

"I don't know what to do. I just don't feel well today."

Suggest walking. Say you're planning to walk a little bit and would they like to come along. Say that you'd like the company. Walking builds the appetite, it feels active, it energizes, it soothes, and having someone want your company feels pretty good, too.

If they are persistent, ask what is bothering them? Does something hurt? What hurts? Where? Ask them to point to it. Then you can check with staff to see if they've mentioned it earlier. You may be told that this is a common complaint. Or you may be told that the problem was checked into earlier. Or you may be thanked for alerting them to it.

The people you visit may complain that nothing is going right, that there is nothing to do, that they are tired of being here, that all they do is sit. Again, acknowledge their truth. Acknowledge their feelings. If you are still working yourself, talk about how it seems that people either have too much to do or not enough. That people either spend all their time working or have time on their hands. That there doesn't seem to be a middle ground. That you, at least, have never found the balance. This gives an opportunity for shared shaking of heads, for laughter, for common ground.

And it gives you the opportunity to follow up with statements like this:

* "Sometimes it seems that all you can do is just put one foot in front of the other."

* "Some days things work, and some days things don't. All we can do is keep going."

The important thing, the helpful thing, is that you are both now talking from the same place. This observation, this insight, this experience, is something you both share. This feeling of sharing, this feeling that you understand, gives the person you visit validation for her feelings as well as a feeling of being connected to you. Validation and connection to other people are two of the most life-enhancing experiences there are. They create light where there is darkness. Fullness where there is emptiness. Openness where things felt closed. Dignity when it seemed to be slipping away.

"Are you going to be here tonight?"

Chances are you are not planning to spend the night. Simply say, "No, I just came to visit you." Just answer it the same way every time it comes up. You can add phrases such as: "But I plan to stay for a while" or "I really enjoy talking with you" or "I've really been looking forward to seeing you" or "I'd really enjoy taking a walk. Do you feel up to walking a little with me?"

"Will you stay with me? Will you be my roommate?"

You can answer, "I'd love to, but you already have a roommate." You may have to go find that roommate and reintroduce them. You may have to do this several times. If both of their names are on the door, point that out. Talk about how you've met the roommate and how nice the person is. Or say that you'd enjoy meeting his roommate.

"I'm not hungry. I don't want to go eat. If I can't go home, I'm not going to eat."

Talk about keeping up their strength. Talk about how they'll lose energy and strength and make it more difficult to get home and get around at home if they don't eat. Ask if it would be all right for you to join them for the meal. Say that you would welcome the companionship.

If this doesn't work at first, drop the subject. If you have the time, say you'd love to wait for a while so you can join them for the meal, and ask if that would be okay. If you can't stay much longer, say you would have loved to wait until both your stomachs were growling, but you have something you need to do; however, add that you hope next time you see each other that you'll be able to eat together. This gives the "not hungry" people something to think about. Do all this lovingly and with a lot of warmth. Some people will eat in order to get the companionship.

If they refuse to eat, don't push. If they get hungry later, they'll mention it to someone. The staff should save a plate and give it to them then. If the food doesn't appeal that day, maybe a nutritional supplement could be offered. It comes in flavors, and chocolate is a common favorite. However, since diets are often directed by a physician, check with the staff to make sure it's okay.

If you know foods the person particularly likes, or a staff member is familiar with their favorite foods, ask if any are available. Make it seem special, and it will be.

"You're just humoring me. You always say that. You're not really giving me answers."

This is a tough one, because they could be right. They recognize you are being noncommittal, that you are dodging their question or demand. Be honest. Say something like "Sometimes I just don't know what to say." Be rueful. You could even add, "Does that ever happen to you?"

You could also say the following: "There are so many things I wish I knew how to do, but I just don't. All I can say is that I keep on learning, and I keep on trying. I'm so sorry I can't do as good a job as you'd like. Can you forgive me?"

Or, instead of asking for forgiveness, tell them that you really like them and enjoy their company, that you are glad you know them.

You need to acknowledge the justice of their remarks and respond to what they are feeling. (This approach is discussed more fully in chapter 1. It might be helpful to flip back.)

"I don't know what's happening to me. I can't seem to remember anything!"

This would be scary for anyone. Don't dismiss it. Acknowledge it. Say, "It's scary, isn't it?" Give them a chance to talk about it. Commiserate with them. Try to gauge whether it is helping them to vent or getting them more upset. This will not only vary from person to person, it will vary from time to time for a particular person. If it seems to be upsetting them more than helping them, take control of the conversation. Be reassuring.

* "Don't force it. You'll think of it later."

* "Don't force it. Sometimes it works better if you do something else for a while."

* "Forcing it never works for me. Relaxing and thinking about something else, or doing something else, works better."

* "Let's do something else for a while. Chances are it'll come to mind when you and I aren't trying so hard."

* "Memory is a trickster. It won't cooperate when we're frustrated. Ever notice that? I know I have."

* "Memory is a tease. Like little boys that pull your hair and then look at you all innocent. You have to pretend you don't care. Not give them any satisfaction."

Then change the subject, or suggest doing something or going somewhere else.

"I don't know what to do; I don't have any money with me."

Part of being an adult is knowing you have money with you. Money stands for independence, flexibility, safety. When we have money, we feel we can buy food, clothing, shelter; get the car fixed if it breaks down; make an impulse purchase; get help; get away. In short, money is one of the chief means we have in modern life to feel we control what happens in our daily lives.

So being concerned about not having money can be a general concern and fear, as well as a specific one. Specific concerns about not having money relate to not being able to pay for meals, not being able to pay for a room for the night, not being able to pay for a bus, train, or taxi to get home.

If the question is general, you can try these approaches:

* "I don't know what happened to it; maybe we could go look."

* "Do you think it might be in your room?"

* "Did you change handbags?" (Ask this only if she's holding one.)

* "Don't worry about it. Everything's all set."

* "Everything here is paid for already."

* "Everything here is paid for already, so you're okay for the time being."

If the question is specific, the approach is similar:

* "You're all set."

* "Your lunch is paid for."

* "Your room is paid for for tonight, so you're okay."

* "It's all taken care of. Isn't that great?"

"Please help me. Can someone please help me?"

These cries are painful to hear. There is such desperation. They may not be coming from someone you are visiting. But if you stop to ask how you can help, often all the person can do is repeat his pleas without being more specific. If the requests are specific, and it's something you can do, by all means do it. If it turns out to be a demand discussed earlier in this section, handle it appropriately. If it is a request you don't know how to handle, or don't know if you should fulfill, either say you'll check to see what you can do, or ask if she'd like to go with you to find out.

Many times it will not be possible to do what people ask. Even though it will be painful for you to find that you won't be able to give them what they want, don't think that you haven't been helpful. It will mean something to them that you cared enough to stop to ask. That you cared enough to find out if this was possible. That you appeared to try to work something out with a staff member. You cared, you gave attention, you tried. That is meaningful.

How will you know you made a difference? Sometimes they will thank you. When you see them another day, they may approach you specifically to make their request, not just call out generally to anyone who might listen. Though they won't know who you are, or remember the previous incident, they will have a memory of your having cared. And your effort will not have been wasted.

Chapter 4

Do's and Don'ts

Learning the Language of Dignity

Life is denied by lack of attention, whether it be to cleaning windows or trying to write a masterpiece.

—Nadia Boulanger

Everything comes down to a simple question you can ask yourself: Will this make my loved one more comfortable or less comfortable?

If you ask a question that requires retrieving something from memory, it's going to make people with Alzheimer's uncomfortable. This means *they* can ask *you* for information, but it's best *you* don't ask *them*.

But it's not just about memory. Much is related to their need to make sense of who they are, where they are, how this new world works and, sometimes, why they are there. This is the life work of small children, but it is much harder for people with Alzheimer's and related conditions. It's always harder to learn new things as we get older. But in this case, there are things they remember, habits that are ingrained, and a feeling of how things are supposed to be, that they can no longer count on. This is compounded by their caretakers not letting them do things that they're used to being able to do. When formerly independent, thriving, resourceful adults perceive this, they find it humiliating. And there are the characteristics of the disease, itself, that not only explain why they are in this situation, but contribute to their not being able to easily make sense of how day-to-day life works. That's scary.

If things suddenly didn't make sense to you, if it seemed there was no logic to what you could do and what you couldn't, what people allowed you to do and what they didn't, what things had what consequences, and what remedies might be available, you'd be searching, shaky, and off-balance, too.

Here are some do's and don'ts.

Don'ts

Don't ask what they ate for lunch.

Don't ask what time it is, unless they still wear a watch and like to use it.

Don't ask what they did today.

Don't ask what they'd like to do now; make a suggestion instead.

Don't ask where they bought their clothes.

Don't ask the name of the person sitting next to them.

Don't ask them to tell you what your name is, or how you are related to them.

Don't bring other names into the conversation without explaining who they are.

Don't say, "You just told me that."

Don't say, "I already know that."

Don't ask, "What kind of music do you like?"

Don't ask if they want to watch a particular show.

Don't say, "We talked about this last time."

Don't say, "I just explained that."

Do's

Do say, "Thanks for telling me."

Do say, "What a nice color that is!"

Do say, "It's nice to see you."

Do say, "I really enjoy talking with you."

Do say, "Can I visit you again?"

Do indicate a commonality of interest; for example, if someone talks about being a teacher, and you have done any teaching, talk about it.

Do ask if they want to watch some television.

Do say, "Do you want to see what's going on over there? Let's check it out."

Do say, "I'm going to walk for a while. Would you like to walk with me?"

Do say, "I wish I could be as feisty as you." Or "as caring," "funny," "strong," "tough"—something true of them and true of your feelings.

Do say, "You have such a great sense of humor."

Do be sincere—they'll feel it if you are not.

Do be patient.

Do let them be a host/hostess.

Do let them be a parent—instruct, give advice, gently admonish.

Do let them talk about their profession—many will think they are still practicing it.

Do honor them for their knowledge, their wisdom, their decisions.

Do thank them for their advice, their insights, their kindnesses.

In general, don't be patronizing or condescending. Be respectful. Treat them as you would want to be treated; they will respond to it.

Some Other Things You Can Do

Bring music they particularly liked at one time, and a way to play it. Don't make them try to remember having liked it by saying you brought it because it was their favorite. Just say you brought some music to listen to while you talk, and ask if they'd like to listen. If they start singing along, or comment how much they like it, then say how glad you are, how you like it, too, and how you hoped they'd like it. Then bring it again another time.

Do the same with books. If you're visiting a parent and there's a book he read to you as a child, over and over—especially a picture book—bring it, and say how you remember liking it a lot and would like to read it again. Would he mind?

Photograph albums are tricky. Names, faces, and relationships become hard to recall, particularly as the disease progresses. You might want to bring a photo album from when the person's children were small—with everyone looking as they did then—and go through that. Often, people with Alzheimer's believe they are living in a different decade. The past is their present. All the years from then to now haven't happened yet, so they can only recognize people they know by how they looked then.

If the photo album has captions, all the better. If not, consult other family members about making labels for the photos. Don't start sentences with "remember when. . . ?" Instead, comment on what's happening in the photo, or on hairstyle, clothes, or something easy to relate to literally. Also, be sure to protect your memories. If you want to leave the album behind, make sure you have a copy made. It would be sad if this family treasure got mislaid.

If they loved gardening or flowers, bring florist and seed catalogs. If they loved furniture, bring catalogs or magazines that picture different styles, different arrangements. Bring something to leaf through, not read.

Take something that you know fits with an old interest of theirs, but act as if it is one of yours. If they remember and love what you brought, great. If not, they are not put on the spot and embarrassed.

More Do's and Don'ts

Sometimes it's helpful to see do's and don'ts side by side. This list expands on the previous ones.

Don't Say	Do Say
What did you have for lunch today?	How was lunch today?
What time is it?	The day's really going by, isn't it?
What did you do today?	How's it going?
Was today rough?	How was your day? Same old same old?
What would you like to do, now?	Would you like to take a walk?
Is that a new sweater?	What a nice sweater. I don't remember it.
Who's that sitting over there?	That person looks nice. Let's go meet him.
Do you know who I am?	Hi, I'm glad to see you.

Don't Say	Do Say
You just told me that.	That's interesting; I didn't know that.
I already know that.	Thanks for telling me.
What kind of music do you like?	Want to go listen to some music?
Do you want to watch *Wheel of Fortune*?	How about seeing if there's anything good on television?
We talked about this last time.	That sounds interesting. I'd like to know more about it.
I just explained that.	Let me show you.
I know how to do that.	That's a good idea. Thanks for telling me. I will have to try it.
Why do you always have a comeback?	I wish I could come up with quick answers like you do. I never think of them until the next day.
I'm an adult, not a child.	You always look out for me. I love you for it.

Don't Say	Do Say
I don't understand why you say things like that.	I'm not sure I got that. Could you explain it again?
What did you do all day?	Did you have a regular day, today?
Did you get your hair done?	Your hair looks great today.
What kind of work did you do?	You must have been good at your work.
Are there any activities tonight?	Let's go see if there are any activities.
What's going on over there?	I wonder what that sound is. Want to check it out? Want to walk over and see?
Have you been sitting there awhile?	You look comfortable. Can I join you?
Did you eat yet?	How was dinner?
How many times have you walked up and down?	Looks like you are getting a lot of walking in. Can I join you?

Don't Say	Do Say
Have you been walking all day?	It looks like *you've* been doing a lot of walking. I'll bet you're in better shape than I am! I've got a lot of walking to do to catch up to you!
How did you think of that?	What a good idea. I wish I'd thought of that.
Why are you asking me that?	That's an interesting question. I hadn't thought about it before.
You asked me that already!	I really don't know, what do you think?
You know I can't do that. Why do you keep asking me?	I wish I could, but I just can't.
Please stop doing that.	You know, I'd really like to stretch my legs. Would you like to join me?

When you say something like "your hair looks really great, today" or "you must have been good at your work," you leave the door wide open for a number of responses without putting people on the spot. A simple "thank you" is all they need to say. This is because you made a comment; you didn't ask a question.

On the other hand, your comment may prompt them to talk about their new hair style, say they just had their hair done, or talk in general about how they loved their work, or how they worked long hours, or how people were satisfied with what they did, or even talk about what kind of work it was they did. But, in case they don't remember what kind of work they did, or they can't remember the right word for it, your comment doesn't force them to admit it to you. This is important.

Helping them maintain their dignity—making sure you don't put them in an awkward position—is the crux of the visit.

Chapter 5

Taking Care of You
Keeping Yourself Whole

We crucify ourselves between two thieves: regret for yesterday and fear for tomorrow.

—Fulton Oursler

The best thing you can do is enjoy the time you have together, and enjoy the other parts of your life.

Types of Visitors

There are five kinds of visitors: family members, friends and coworkers, formal volunteers, informal visitors who come frequently, and family members who visit rarely or not at all. Most things in this book apply to the first four pretty equally.

In general, visits are more difficult emotionally for family members and friends than for volunteers and strangers. The obvious reason is that the people you love have changed, and it's painful to see them differently. But there are other reasons. It is also because unresolved issues are still very much there and you fear that you may have lost your chance to resolve them. It is also because you feel guilty that you couldn't help them get better and you had to take them away from a familiar environment. And it is also because, even when they can't remember their relationship to you or even your name, they may know that there *is* a relationship, and they may let you feel their anger, their resentment, their despair more than they would show it to someone else.

Visits are also difficult for volunteers and informal visitors. If you don't know much about the background or interests of the people you are visiting, it's hard to guess what is accurate in their conversation and what isn't. That makes it tricky to know how to react.

Why Do Some Family Members Not Visit?

There may be any number of reasons that family members don't visit. Some are the same as the reasons that you *do* visit. You come because you hope you can help, because you hope you can resolve unresolved issues, because you feel guilty, because you know you are needed, or at least hope so. Those who don't come feel they can't help, are afraid of unresolved issues, feel guilty, and are either not sure they are needed or doubt they can meet the need. In addition, they either don't know how to handle the situation, or are sure they can't, and don't realize they can learn. Sometimes it's simply pain—that they may give another name— that stops them.

There is no way to force people to visit. All you can do is accept that they are the way they are and hope it will change down the road. You can give them reports from time to time on how it's going. You can let them realize from what you say that it gets easier with practice and experience, and that there are opportunities for closeness and for laughter and for a new kind of relationship. You don't need to say these things straight out; let your anecdotes and stories speak for themselves. They will be able to read between the lines.

If you can do that, you will feel less resentment that they don't go. Think of them as just not being ready. Think of them as being in their own form of pain. Don't begrudge the time you spend. When the person you are visiting dies, and you can no longer visit, something will be missing. But at least you'll know you went. Those who didn't visit will always wonder what they missed.

Supporting People Who Visit

If you find it difficult to spend time with loved ones who suffer from Alzheimer's, there are ways you can help your friends and relatives who do visit. Instead of feeling guilty or resentful that they are able to do this and you can't, instead of letting them make you feel guilty or resentful, thank them for doing it and offer to support them in other areas of their lives. It takes time and energy to go. Find ways to give them the gift of time and energy. Run errands for them from time to time; cook an occasional meal or pick up their groceries; baby-sit for their children so they can go out and renew themselves with a night out. Show your appreciation in tangible ways: send them a card with thanks for their efforts; bring them something meaningful you know they'd appreciate—flowers, candy, a book, music, or a treat they don't usually allow themselves.

Don't let your not visiting create a rift. People have different personalities, different talents, different abilities. Maybe someday visiting will be something you can do; in the meantime, support the people who are doing it, and listen to them when they tell you about how it's going.

Asking for Help

Visiting, especially in the beginning, before you have learned to live in the moment, can be draining as well as time-consuming. Ask for help. Rearrange and reassign the chores in your household. Reexamine all the things you do and figure out which don't need to be done, which can be done less often, and which can be done by someone else.

When you carve out time to visit, make sure you also carve out time to recharge yourself. Just fifteen minutes each day doing something you wouldn't normally do for yourself will pay tremendous dividends. Take a few minutes from watching television, or from opening junk mail, or from making a phone call just to vent. Instead, make a milk shake and relax in a chair you don't usually sit in, make a bubble bath instead of taking a shower, put on some music that you don't usually listen to, go for a walk, have someone give you a massage, put some cinnamon in a pot of boiling water and just enjoy the smell, or start rereading a book you always liked.

Another thing you can do is change the way you are thinking about the person you are visiting. Write down the three things you always liked best about him. Write down the three things he always liked best in you. Maybe write down the three best experiences you had together. The list is endless. And the best list is the one you generate. Talk to a childhood friend about all the things you used to like to do, to watch, to listen to. Brainstorm. Between that list and this one, you'll have a start at finding things that will refresh you. Just brainstorming will count for one night.

Make sure you keep fun in your life—or if you've misplaced it, that you put it back in.

Visitors and Volunteers

Creating a distinction between staff and visitors is important. There are two reasons for this. One is that it protects the visitor. There are times when you will need to pass the buck because there are things you can't provide or agree to. If the person you care about recognizes (or is reminded) that you don't work here, that you cannot make this decision, your "no" will be accepted. (See chapter 2 for more on this.)

The other reason is that it enhances the time you spend together. People know the difference between staff and visitors. The interaction with a staff person can be warm, loving, humorous, enjoyable, caring—but it is still understood that the person is doing a job. Does it matter that the person is doing her job well? That she shows how much she cares? That she takes the time to talk one-on-one?

Of course. It matters a lot. But the awareness is still there that this relationship is professional, not personal. It is important for people to feel that someone is visiting them because they care about them personally. That he is not there because he works there. That he has made a special trip because he cares about them and enjoys their company.

Creating a distinction between staff and visitor is not the only distinction to consider. Often, there is a blurring of the boundary between visitor and volunteer. This can be unfortunate. Being a volunteer is often a formal arrangement—with regular hours, duties, and responsibilities. Volunteers often have the responsibility to arrange entertainment, run bingo games, deliver services, such as getting people places, serving special snacks, providing music, and organizing events. This is not true of people who simply drop by to visit people they didn't previously know.

If you come to visit and provide companionship, on your own schedule or whim, with no other parameters at all, you need to reinforce that. Remind them that you come just to visit them, to spend time, to talk; remind them that you don't work there, that this is not your job, that you have a different job somewhere else. Ask staff not to introduce you as a volunteer; explain that you feel that word is distancing—that it can be viewed as good works, patronizing, not personal in nature—and that using it can make a difference in the effect you can achieve.

Visitors Who Are New to the People They Visit

One of the great things about being a visitor, and being perceived a stranger, is the feeling of a fresh start you can give to the person you visit. If they haven't met you before, there is nothing they need to remember. There is no room for embarrassment or humiliation or frustration. There is no need to work very hard to fake any kind of knowledge. There is no chance of being confused by what you say. Instead, people can fall back on all the social graces and conversational gambits they've used all their lives when they meet new people. They can ask questions knowing they are not expected to know the answers. This is liberating and enjoyable and relaxing. It is an oasis in the middle of so many other memory-taxing situations. And it renews a sense of self-respect and dignity.

Frequency and Length of Visits

Don't lock yourself in a mindset. Some people think they need to spend an hour each time they go. Some people think they need to go every week without fail.

Regularity is important. Long gaps between visits become more and more problematic as a person's condition worsens. But only you can determine how often you can visit. And the people you visit won't remember exactly when you were last there. The important thing is to make visits frequent enough so they can remember they know you—even if they don't know who you are.

So, if you decide to start visiting someone who doesn't know you, and you want him to remember seeing you before and that seeing you was enjoyable, you may want to go very frequently in the first two or three weeks and establish a memory. Going at least three times a week during that period will work with a lot of people. After that, dropping back won't matter. You will need to judge this for yourself with the person you are visiting. If you don't go at all for an entire week or two, you may find you need to step up the frequency for the next ten days and reestablish the memory. But if you are content to be perceived as someone new each time you go, that's fine, too.

Length of visit matters very little. If you can go twice a week for ten minutes, you may do as much good, maybe more, than if you go once a week for an hour. You'll have shown up, and you will have made a connection; your face and voice and touch will have registered.

You do what you can do. And if it comes to the point where the person you visit thinks you are a stranger each time you come, remember that there are benefits to that, too. If you convey a sense of not being rushed, of living in the moment with her, of being glad you are there with her, it won't matter how long you stay. And all this can be achieved in a few minutes.

What's important is the connection. What's important is the one-on-one. What's important is that you "come whole" to those meetings. If you take care of yourself, both you and everyone around you will benefit.

Rewards

If you put the disease in the background and the person in the foreground, always remembering who he is, then you will be like the sun shining light toward him and he will shine light back on you.

When people don't know who you are, or any outer world things about you, they will only see *you*. They may be the only people who can do that. Who else enjoys your company without knowing their relationship with you, without knowing what kind of work you do, without knowing your economic situation or your social status, without knowing if your life is happy or sad? When you are with them, you are stripped to your essence. Most people are distracted, seduced, blinded by everything else and don't see you. But the people you visit are not most people. They love you and appreciate you and respect you for who you really are. This is a great gift they can give *you*.

Chapter 6

Moving Toward Joy
Helping Your Children Visit

Laughter is the valve on the pressure cooker of life. You either laugh at stuff or you end up with your brains or your beans on the ceiling.

—Wavy Gravy

Helping your children visit is all about making them comfortable. Children need to know that the biggest thing is just being there. That's their gift to the person they are visiting. It's not what they say or what they do or what they show.

What matters is that grandma or grandpa can feel that the children are happy to see them. That will make them happy.

It's all about giving joy. There are so many simple ways in which children can do this. They can say how happy they are to see grandma. They can say, "I'm glad to be here." They can say, "I've missed you." They can say, "I love you."

But words are not required. Children can smile. They can sit or squat next to their grandparents and just look up and listen. They can hold their grandparents' hands or lean into them or on them.

They can show something: perhaps an old photo album that shows grandpa as a young man with his parents or his children when they were small. Perhaps something they've made recently—a drawing, a school project, a card made specially for grandpa.

They can provide entertainment. They can bring an instrument, juggle balls, do magic tricks, twirl batons, make paper airplanes. It doesn't really matter. Grandparents take pleasure and pride in watching young people perform, and they will always think it's splendid.

They can talk about their own lives. They can talk about the baseball game they played, or the hockey game they watched; they can talk about a movie they saw or the sleepover party they enjoyed. It's not what you talk about that is important; it's the talking itself. It's being together that counts.

They can talk about the weather. Maybe it was so windy that they almost got knocked over. That's something to wonder at and laugh about. And that brings up an important thing for children to understand. Though the situation is serious, the visit should not be. The visit should be about happiness and fun. And if children tell very simple jokes and laugh at them, even if their grandparents don't get the joke, the joy and laughter is contagious. "Isn't that funny?" the grandchild could say. "I really like that joke. It always makes me laugh."

These are things children do very well. At the same time, they may have some concerns, and even some fears. Talking to your children about them can be of enormous help.

Questions You May Have

"What are my child's unspoken concerns?"

Some of your child's unspoken concerns are the same as yours: "I don't know what to do. I don't know what to say. It hurts to see grandma this way. What if she doesn't understand what I say? What if she is crying all the time? What if she doesn't even know who I am?"

"What are the concerns my child doesn't even realize he has?"

Your child is dealing with fear, uncertainty, and loss of control. One of the things children look forward to—it's part of the business of childhood—is growing up. The key thing they associate with adulthood is freedom. They see adulthood as the time when they'll finally have some control over their lives. Adulthood, freedom, and control are all tied together.

Yet now they see adults that they love and admire losing control, losing independence, losing relationships, and becoming subject to other adults. This is scary.

It is scary because it is not what adulthood means to them. On the one hand, they can really identify with their grandparents because they know what it is like not to have control over their lives. On the other hand, they don't want to face what's happening because it goes against everything they are working toward in their own lives. They don't want to see adulthood as a time of illness, death, and mental deterioration.

They have to struggle with these fears for themselves, which they may not even be admitting to themselves. And they have to deal with these fears on top of the pain of seeing people they love losing so much.

Another thing that children spend their childhood doing is figuring out who they are. It's particularly the business of teenagers to create their own identity, to separate themselves from their parents, to develop a sense of independence, autonomy, and discipline, to create new relationships with their parents as well as other people. So it is particularly difficult for teenagers to visit their grandparents in this situation—because everything their grandparents are experiencing seems to be life running in reverse. It's as if a movie is running backwards for the adults while for the teens it is going forward. This is more than jarring.

"What can I say to my child?"

You might want to bring these fears out into the open. You might want to talk about the pain. Children often feel that visiting will make them feel worse; this is not necessarily true. If they visit and bring some joy, bring some feeling of connection, the pain can become easier to handle. Making a difference for a grandparent can bring joy to the grandchild. And there is no question that grandchildren can make a difference. Those are the favorite visits.

You can reassure them. It's very difficult to "blow" a visit. Unless they make a point of telling their grandparents that they hate them, that they don't want to visit them, that they wish they were the way they used to be—or they sulk and refuse to say anything at all—their visits will be welcomed and enjoyed and do a lot of good.

Talking and connecting can be difficult in the first visits. Make sure children have something to show or do, particularly with their hands. A young child can bring a doll or a truck and play with it and talk about it. An older child can bring a Rubik's Cube or a Slinky. A pet is always a good icebreaker. Having something to do that they can also talk about makes things comfortable for everyone. And it has the added benefit of being something to talk about that is grounded in the present moment—no worries about asking grandparents to remember something from the past.

Teens need to know they have decades of adulthood to look forward to, with various degrees of independence and control over their lives. They need to know that they are unlikely to face what their grandparent is facing, but that if it does happen, it's far into the future. Furthermore, by then, research may have uncovered ways to prevent the disease as well as treat it. They need to know that they have a lot to give their grandparents, and the chief thing is their love, which they can show by spending time with them, even if it is silent companionship. Even if it is just sitting nearby and doing homework and looking up every so often to smile or squeeze a hand.

Chapter 7

Second Impressions
Reintroducing a Person

Doctors, Nurses, please beware!
This placid looking patient here
Can teach you how to fly a plane
Or downhill ski in rough terrain!

—extracted from a poem by
Margaret V. Ross that was
posted in her father-in-law's
room for staff to see

One of the things that separates visitor from staff is memory. You remember how your loved ones were. They can't. How can staff members see the essence of the people they care for until they get to know them? How can they know their accomplishments and what they stand for?

It is not only you who has to keep in mind that this is a person, not a disease. But you have an advantage that staff members don't have. A staff member's first impression is one of illness, dependence, need, confusion. *You* know the strengths of this person, you can remember his vigor, her persistence, his leadership, her pioneering efforts, his football career, her awards.

On my visits, I have met teachers, engineers, businesspeople; those who worked on Wall Street and those who have worked at the Pentagon. I've met beauticians and seamstresses, environmental engineers, and designers. One person worked for the CIA and another designed clothes for a famous actress. Some raised many children, all of whom made a place for themselves in the world. And those are the few who could tell me about their lives (which others verified for me). None of these kinds of accomplishments and career choices are evident on their faces. Most don't talk about them much, if at all. The best thing is to assume that everyone you meet has had a creative and constructive and rewarding and giving life.

When you think of someone this way, you automatically treat him differently. It's human nature. You will accord her respect. You will have more patience. You will protect the dignity of the people you meet and know.

Staff members will be grateful for any help you can give them with this. It's much easier to work from knowledge than it is from imagination. The same thing that separates visitors from staff also separates staff from the people they care for: they don't have memories to draw from. We can't give staff members our memories; but we can give them information.

When we do that, their perspective shifts. It's like holding up a kaleidoscope and turning the lens slightly. Things look different. There is color, brightness, beauty.

Hand them a kaleidoscope and you will change everyone's world.

Chapter 8

Some Extra Tips
Making Visits Count

Men hate those to whom they have to lie.

—Victor Hugo

Lying hurts. This is another argument for sincerity, respect, love, and dignity. Lying not only hurts the person you are visiting, it not only hurts the relationship you have, it also hurts you. What could be more harmful to you than being consumed by hatred? What could be more harmful to you than hating the people you love?

If you haven't read chapter 1 carefully, or you haven't thought about emotional truths, go back and revisit it. The older people get, the better they are at smelling sincerity, tasting sincerity, feeling it in their heart and soul and bones. If you are sincere, the person you visit will know.

And you will know.

Good luck through this whole process. Find ways to enjoy it together. And remember, once the people you love are far down the path, they will be unable to remember the pain of the past and unable to fear the pain of the future. They will only be able to feel the pain or joy of the present. You can help them make that joy.

One way is to emphasize that you are a visitor. But, in addition to making sure they understand that your spending time with them is not a matter of obligation (because you are not a staff member), and that you are there because you want to be and because you enjoy their company, it is important that they believe they deserve to spend time with you and are giving something back.

Make Them Feel They Are Giving You Something

Relationships are two-way. And it's uncomfortable when they are unequal. Find ways for the person you are visiting to feel that *you* are benefiting from the relationship and the time together.

You can try saying things like this:

* "This is so relaxing, sitting here with you."

* "I don't know how you do it, but you always make me laugh."

* "I haven't laughed this much all day. Thanks."

* "I enjoy your company so much."

* "That's great advice. I'll have to use it."

* "That's interesting. I'm going to want to think about that."

* "We never had time to just sit around like this before. This is nice."

* "With all that walking, you get more exercise than I do. I'm going to have to try to follow your example."

* "You are always so calm. I hope I can learn from you."

* "Your smile always makes my day."

* "I never knew that. That's great."

Don't Assume

Even though much of this book focuses on not challenging people's memories about who they are or where they are or *when* they are, try to avoid making assumptions about what they can still do or what they can still enjoy.

For example, there may be games they can play besides bingo. Maybe they would enjoy a card game such as Go Fish or Old Maid, or a simple follow-the-path board game such as Candyland.

Perhaps they would still enjoy reading a short story or a *National Geographic* magazine, or even enjoy having someone read something to them. It may not be necessary for them to remember the whole story at the end; they may just enjoy the flow, the action at the moment, the sound of the words washing over them. It doesn't matter what part of it they like, or if they can explain it to you; all that matters is that they derive enjoyment from it.

Pay Attention to Tone

Remember, your tone of voice is more important than the content of your words. Body language, gestures, touch, smiles, and sincerity all make your loved ones feel that they are being taken seriously, that they are still loved, still worthy of respect, still adults. That is what you strive for. That is the gift you bring.

Afterword

I have focused on people living in an assisted-living situation, whether in their own homes or as part of a retirement community. Much of this book also applies to visiting people in nursing homes, but there are some additional communication issues as people become less and less verbal and less and less physically independent. The scope of communication approaches becomes narrower, with touch and body language becoming more and more important, as people lose the ability to process even the most everyday words and phrases.

I focused on assisted-living situations because it is the middle ground between some functioning at home and the intensive care needed in nursing homes. The assisted-living situation is where everything begins to get difficult, where visits drop off, where pain and discomfort and a sense of being visited by strangers begins. It's a turning point for all the family members, whether they are the ones now living in a secure unit, or whether they are the ones who had to arrange it, or whether they are simply the ones left behind.

Once you have spent time with a family member in an assisted-living situation, you will have become familiar with different behaviors and ways to handle them. By the time you get to the point where he has to leave assisted living—because things have deteriorated greatly—you will have learned a lot and adjusted gradually. What is in this book is not a blueprint; it is a start for those new to the situation or hesitant to walk into it. Responding to the various issues, situations, behaviors, questions, comments, and demands is very individual, and you have to make a lot of it up as you go along. However, if you have skipped the whole assisted-living phase, and only start visiting at the nursing home stage, this book can still provide suggestions and background.

The whole idea of writing this book was to make it easier for people to visit, and to encourage those who are fortunate enough not to have family members or friends suffering in this way to do so also. As difficult as it is to do in the beginning, it can become a very rewarding part of your life.

Resources

Your best resources are the other people who have walked this road before you. Here are the best ways to find them, and some of the materials they have developed along the way.

Organizations

There are several key organizations with knowledgeable people who will spend time with you on the phone or via e-mail.

Alzheimer's Association
919 North Michigan Avenue, Suite 1100
Chicago, IL 60611-1676
(800) 272-3900
www.alz.org
info@alz.org

The contact center is open around the clock, and social workers on staff are available for consultation between 3:00 P.M. and 8:00 A.M., 365 days a year. E-mail is checked daily, and the Web site has links to local chapters.

This is the national organization; hundreds of chapters across the country provide support and information about resources in your area. These chapters will also connect you with other people in your situation, people who have been going through what you are now facing and can help you find your way through it. Ask for information related to communication and relationships.

ADEAR Center
National Institute on Aging
P.O. Box 8250
Silver Spring, MD 20907-8250
(800) 438-4380
www.alzheimers.org
adear@alzheimers.org

This is the Alzheimer's Disease Education and Referral Center, which is part of the National Institutes of Health. The phone is manned from 8:30 A.M. to 5:00 P.M. weekdays. Information specialists will respond to e-mail during the same hours. If you send e-mail over the weekend, depending on the volume, the specialists will usually be able to answer by Monday afternoon or Tuesday morning.

Eldercare Locator
(800) 677-1116
www.aoa.dhhs.gov

This program provides national directory assistance to help you find local area agencies on aging and other community resources. It is a service of the Administration on Aging (AOA) in the U.S. Department of Health and Human Services. The phone lines are covered weekdays, from 9:00 A.M. to 8:00 P.M. The AOA Web site has a chart with a number of helpful linked services, one of which is Eldercare Locator.

National Parkinson's Foundation, Inc.
Bob Hope Parkinson Research Center
1501 N.W. Ninth Avenue
Bob Hope Road
Miami, FL 33136-1494
(800) 327-4545
www.parkinson.org
mailbox@parkinson.org

This organization provides information and medical support. Two nurses answer the phone from 9:00 A.M. to 5:00 P.M. weekdays; there is an answering machine for the weekend, and calls are routed to the appropriate person for return calls on Monday morning. Dr. Abraham Lieberman, the medical director and a nationally known movement disorders specialist, answers specific questions on treatment options and current care via e-mail; this is an anonymous forum, and access to it is through the "ask the doctor" column on the foundation's Web site.

National Stroke Association
9707 E. Easter Lane
Englewood, CO 80112
(800) STROKES; (303) 649-9299
www.stroke.org

This organization offers information via the Web site and by mail, and provides referrals to local stroke support groups. A phone line is manned from 7:30 A.M. to 5:00 P.M. weekdays, and you can make contact via e-mail on the Web site; expect a response within twenty-four hours.

National Association of Professional Geriatric Care
   Managers (GCM)
1604 N. Country Club Road
Tucson, AZ 85716-33102
(520) 881-8008
www.caremanager.org
info@caremanager.org

If you are looking to hire someone to help you manage the process, this is a place to start. A professional geriatric care manager can help with assessing what kind of care your loved one needs, determine eligibility for assistance, screen and monitor in-home help, review financial/medical/legal issues, refer you to medical professionals, assist with crisis intervention, and help with liaisons if you live in one state and your loved one lives somewhere else. This association has members with various levels of training in different areas, including nursing, social work, psychology, human services, and gerontology. To find people with the training you want in your local area, consult the Web site or order a directory.

Newsletters and Magazines

The Caregiver. A newsletter published by the Duke Family Support Program, Box 3600, Duke Medical Center, Durham, NC 27710. This newsletter provides tips for caregivers, summaries of recent research, information on new resources—in print, on the Web, through associations—and a forum for caregivers to share their thoughts, suggestions, and experiences. $10 per year; free for people living in North Carolina. Call (800) 672-4213 or (919) 660-7510.

Take Care!, a free newsletter for family caregivers (there is a fee for professionals, paid providers, and organizations). It is sponsored by the National Family Caregivers Association, 101400 Connecticut Avenue, #500, Kensington, MD 20895-3944. (800) 896-3650; www.nfcacares.org or info@nfcacares.org.

Today's Caregiver, a magazine for primary and secondary family caregivers, regardless of the disease or situation that makes compassionate care necessary. It was founded by the son of a primary caregiver. It's easy reading and provides support and encouragement. 6365 Taft Street, Suite #3004, Hollywood, FL 33024. (800) 829-2734 or (954) 893-0550; www.caregiver.com or info@caregiver.com

Web Sites

http://www.aoa.dhhs.gov/caregivers/default.htm
This is an Administration on Aging site on caregiver resources. It provides a wealth of information and links.

http://www.healthinaging.org
This is a site of the American Geriatrics Society.

www.caregiver.org
This is the Family Caregiver Alliance (FCA) site. It has an online support group as part of the Web site and an "Ask the Expert" column both through e-mail and the Web site. A professional answers within forty-eight hours. Within California, the FCA has a model program that helps people find placement, refers them to agencies if they want in-home care, and offers a respite program. In 2002, they will be starting a National Center on Caregiving that will be a resource for caregivers nationwide. You can reach the FCA directly at (415) 434-3388, (800) 445-8106 (toll free in California), or at info@caregiver.org, or write to 690 Market Street, Suite 600, San Francisco, CA 94104. The FCA covers a broad spectrum of issues and provides specific, helpful information. Regular hours are 9:00 A.M. to 5:00 P.M. weekdays.

www.elderweb.com
Provides links to specific resources in specific states and countries. You can search by region or by topic.

www.va.gov/customer/Eligibility.asp
This is the FAQ page of the U.S. Department of Veterans Affairs site. It provides information and

links on nursing home, medical, and financial support available to veterans within their communities.

www.strokenetwork.org
Provides links to other resources and offers a handbook for caregivers that can be downloaded from the site.

http://www.alz.co.uk/alz/almain.htm
This is the site of Alzheimer's Disease International (ADI). ADI is an umbrella organization for Alzheimer's associations all around the world. It will connect you with associations in fifty-seven countries. You can reach ADI directly at +44 207 620 3011, or by fax at +44 207 401 7351, or by e-mail at info@alz.co.uk, or write to 45/46 Lower Marsh, London, SE1 7RG, United Kingdom. When calling from the U.S., dial 011 before the rest of the number.

From Voices Not Yet Lost

Perspectives, a newsletter for individuals diagnosed with Alzheimer's disease, is written both by and for the diagnosed person. It offers some practical suggestions for coping with Alzheimer's disease and related disorders. Lisa Snyder publishes it quarterly through the Alzheimer's Disease Research Center at the University of California at San Diego in La Jolla, California. The current subscription rate is $24. Call (858) 622-5800 or e-mail lsnyder@ucsd.edu

Snyder, Lisa. 1999. *Speaking Our Minds, Personal Reflections from Individuals with Alzheimer's*. New York: W. H. Freeman and Company Publishers. Available in a large-print edition, in hardcover, and in paperback.

Henderson, Cary Smith. 1998. *Partial View: An Alzheimer's Journal*. Dallas: Southern Methodist University Press. Henderson, a professor, commented on what he was experiencing as his Alzheimer's disease progressed. The photographer is Nancy Anderson.

Helpful Books

Bell, Virginia, and David Troxell. 1997. *The Best Friends Approach to Alzheimer's Care*. Baltimore:

Health Professions Press. Available from Health Professions Press, P.O. Box 10624, Baltimore, MD 21285-0624. This book's philosophy is to look at the whole person.

Fazio, Sam, and Dorothy Seman and Jane Stansell. 1999. *Rethinking Alzheimer's Care.* Baltimore: Health Professions Press.

Gwyther, Lisa P. 2001. *Caring for People with Alzheimer's Disease: A Manual for Facility Staff.* Washington, DC: American Health Care Association; Chicago: Alzheimer's Disease and Related Disorders Association. This is the updated version of *Alzheimer's Patients: A Manual for Nursing Home Staff.* It is designed to help staff understand and care for people suffering from dementia.

Gwyther, Lisa P. 1995. *You Are One of Us: Successful Clergy/Church Connections for Alzheimer's Families.* Durham, NC: Duke University Medical Center. Available from Duke Family Support Program, or from ADEAR at (800) 438-4380. This small book (59 pages) offers helpful tips and approaches for clergy and volunteers who visit, and most of what is in it would be helpful to anyone wanting to communicate effectively and tenderly with people struggling with dementia.

Hellen, Carly. 1992. *Alzheimer's Disease: Activity Focused Care*. Boston: Andover Medical Publishers. A very good resource for people working in the field of dementia, particularly in settings outside the home, and particularly for long-term care.

Mace, Nancy L., and Peter V. Rabins, M.D. 1989, 1999. *The 36-Hour Day: a Family Guide to Caring for Folks with Alzheimer's Disease and Related Dementing Illnesses and Memory Loss in Late Life*. Baltimore: Johns Hopkins University Press.

Robinson, Anne, Beth Spencer, and Laurie White. 1989, 1999. *Understanding Difficult Behaviors: Some Practical Suggestions for Coping with Alzheimer's Disease and Related Disorders*. Ypsilanti, MI: Geriatric Education Center of Michigan. Order by phone at (734) 487-2335. The Web site is www.emich.edu/public/alzheimers

Shanks, Lela. 1996. *Your Name is Hughes Hannibal Shanks: A Caregiver's Guide to Alzheimer's*. Lincoln,

NE: University of Nebraska Press. Shanks shares her experience in caring for her husband at home. She provides tips about adapting the home and where to go for support, and talks about how she helped her children interact more effectively with their father as the disease progressed. She also gives examples of how she created opportunities for meaningful experiences during the course of his illness.

Strauss, Peter J., and Nancy M. Lederman. 1996. *Elder Law Handbook: A Legal and Financial Survival Guide for Caregivers and Seniors*. New York: Facts on File.

Warner, Mark. 1998. *The Complete Guide to Alzheimer Proofing Your Home*. West Lafayette, IN: Purdue University Press.

Especially for Kids

Baumann, Kathy, and Erin Conners. 1995. *Through Tara's Eyes: Helping Children Cope with Alzheimer's Disease*. Rockville, MD: American Health Assistance Foundation. Aimed at children aged five to ten. Available only from the publisher. Call (800) 437-2423.

Fading Memories: An Adolescent's Guide to Alzheimer's Disease. 1997. Rockville, MD: American Health Assistance Foundation. Written by adolescents for adolescents, by middle school students at the Blessed Sacrament School in Virginia, under the direction of Kathy Baumann. Only available directly from the publisher. Call (800) 437-2423.

Fox, M. 1984. *Wilfred Gordon McDonald Partridge.* Brooklyn, NY: Kane/Miller. This book for preschoolers helps parents talk to their children about memory disorders affecting someone they love.

Sakai, Kimiko. 1990. *Sachiko Means Happiness.* Tomie Arai, illustrator. Emeryville, CA: Children's Book Press. Aimed at children four to eight. Available in paperback and hardcover.

Sanford, Doris. *Maria's Grandma Gets Mixed Up.* Graci Evans, illustrator. Portland, OR: Multnomah, 1989. For children aged four to eight. This book features a Latino family. It is not available through bookstores, but your local library can get it through interlibrary loan.

For more books for kids, go to the Web site, www.alz.org, and, using the search function, type in "information for children and adolescents." The list contains both fiction and nonfiction, is organized by age, and gives a summary of each book.

Topic Finder

This section lists different situations, behaviors, issues, demands, and questions that you might encounter, as well as questions *you* might have, and lists them here in the order in which they appear in the book so that you can locate them easily.

Claudia Strauss is an award-winning communication consultant and educator. An adjunct professor of English at Albright College in Reading, PA, Ms. Strauss runs a business in strategic communication, and coaches adults with ADD and learning disabilities. Inspired by the many people with Alzheimer's disease that she has come to know through her frequent visits to a secure dementia unit, Ms. Strauss felt impelled to share her insights into how to communicate more fully and at deeper levels, even as this disease progresses.